"By Grace You Have Been Saved"

Bible Studies on Healing and Reconciliation

"BY GRACE YOU HAVE BEEN SAVED"

*Bible Studies
on Healing
and Reconciliation*

WCC Publications, Geneva

Cover design: Marie Arnaud Snakkers

ISBN 2-8254-1431-X

© 2005 WCC Publications
World Council of Churches
150 route de Ferney, P.O. Box 2100
1211 Geneva 2, Switzerland
Website: http://www.wwc-coe.org

Printed in France

Contents

Foreword

By praying to God's Spirit which renews all things, we confess that mission does not belong to us but that we confidently trust that we are ready to receive, become and share signs of forgiveness and peace as a way of responding responsibly to the mission entrusted to us: to create healing communities and participate in the process of reconciliation by working to overcome all forms of violence.

These Bible studies have been prepared for the world conference on mission and evangelism, held in Athens, Greece, 9-16 May 2005. The aim of the conference is to give participants the means to continue responding to the call made to them to participate together in mission and to work today in God's world for reconciliation and healing in Christ. The liturgical and meditative aspects will be very much part of the conference and a time of *lectio divina* will be practised each day so as to create spaces for speaking, sharing and discussing which allow everyone both to listen to themselves and to discover the treasures of others' traditions. Thus the way the conference has been structured seeks of itself to work towards healing and reconciliation between participants.

The spiritual life committee has published this book as a means of encouraging the theme of the conference to be become part of congregational life. It is intended to be for personal and communal use, both during and after the gathering. The authors come from different traditions and countries and their writing shows both the strength of our unity in Christ and the rich diversity God offers us.

Bible Studies
for Adults

1 *Come, Holy Spirit, Heal and Reconcile!*

Isaiah 11:1-9;
Ezekiel 36:24-28
Kyung-Taek Ha

A shoot shall come out from the stock of Jesse, and a branch shall grow out of his roots. The spirit of the Lord shall rest on him, the spirit of wisdom and understanding, the spirit of counsel and might, the spirit of knowledge and the fear of the Lord. His delight shall be in the fear of the Lord. He shall not judge by what his eyes see, or decide by what his ears hear; but with righteousness he shall judge the poor, and decide with equity for the meek of the earth; he shall strike the earth with the rod of his mouth, and with the breath of his lips he shall kill the wicked. Righteousness shall be the belt around his waist, and faithfulness the belt around his loins. The wolf shall live with the lamb, the leopard shall lie down with the kid, the calf and the lion and the fatling together, and a little child shall lead them. The cow and the bear shall graze, their young shall lie down together; and the lion shall eat straw like the ox. The nursing child shall play over the hole of the asp, and the weaned child shall put its hand on the adder's den. They will not hurt or destroy on all my holy mountain; for the earth will be full of the knowledge of the Lord as the waters cover the sea. (Isa. 11:1-9)

I will take you from the nations, and gather you from all the countries, and bring you into your own land. I will sprinkle clean water upon you, and you shall be clean from all your uncleanness, and from all your idols I will cleanse you. A new heart I will give you, and a new spirit I will put within you; and I will remove from your body the heart of stone and give you a heart of flesh. I will put my spirit within you, and make you follow my statutes and be careful to observe my ordinances. Then you shall live in the land that I gave to your ancestors; and you shall be my people, and I will be your God. (Ezek. 36:24-28)

Isaiah 11:1-9

Question 1: Introduction (What is this text about?)

Isaiah 11:1-9 is a well-known text and, together with Isaiah 9:1-6, contains prophecies of the Messiah. In Isaiah 11:1-9, the hope is expressed for justice and for a kingdom of peace, to be brought about by a future Lord (of the universe), the "Messiah". This text is usually described as an eschatological expectation. But what does the word "eschatology" mean? This text is not an idea of the world beyond our world, but rather *the expectation of a time of salvation in the future*. It is a future which will be different from our present time, which will take place through the lordship of a new ruler. But even though it appears to be a promise for the future, it is already beginning to affect our world here and now.

Question 2: Explanation of the text (What does each element mean?)

1. In Isaiah 11:2 *the nature of the expectant ruler* is revealed. The new ruler is not qualified to rule by a noble descent, like a king, but rather *by the spirit of the Lord*. Three pairs of characteristics are named which express his qualifications more precisely: wisdom and understanding, counsel and might, knowledge and the fear of the Lord. The first two pairs of characteristics could also be the usual qualities of an ideal king. He needs these elements in order to exercise his office properly. For the king to officiate as judge, he requires the characteristics of wisdom and understanding (as for example Solomon did in Kings 3:9). In order to carry out the business of the realm, both internal and external, the king needs this capability (as also counsel and might) to understand situations, make plans and come to the appropriate decisions. What is special about the future Lord is found in the third pair of characteristics. This pair of words is not a traditional element of the ideology of kingship. It is knowledge and the fear of the Lord, which describes the essential practice of a life lived with the Lord. The prophet Hosea, for example, mentions knowledge of the Lord as the decisive event in the relation between human being and God (cf. Hosea 2:20; 4:1b; 6:6). And in the wisdom of Israel, fear of the Lord is represented as the basis for all human conduct (cf. Proverbs 1:7; 9:10; 15:33; Job 28:28). Here we have the words knowledge

and fear of the Lord closely tied together. So we can assume that the new ruler not only knows the will of God, but also carries it out, through his office, in the fear of God.

2. Isaiah 11:3-5 describes the *influence of the awaited ruler*. The one who exercises his rule under the influence of the spirit of the Lord is a ruler who sees that justice is done. He governs his realm quite differently from the way human beings would do it. He does not depend on what his eyes see or what his ears hear. A *transformation of the use of power* is revealed here. The power of the future lord will not be used for military purposes, but rather in order that justice may be done. His justice is implemented to help the powerless obtain their rights. In accordance with the Old Testament idea of God, he appears as the advocate of the poor (Psalms 9:10; 68:6; Job 5:15-16), for the rights of the least powerful. It is striking that his task is carried out through the "rod of his mouth" and the "breath of his lips". These metaphorical expressions reveal the authority of the new ruler's speech. The characteristics of his word are made plain through his prophetic actions: through the words of the (prophet's) mouth, the Lord kills evil-doers (Hos. 6:5). The Lord makes the mouth of his servant like a sharp sword (Isa. 49:2). The word of the Lord shatters rocks like a hammer (Jer. 23:29). Unlike an ordinary king, the new ruler does not have swords or spears as his weapons, but rather *the power of his word*. But this can only happen because his word is founded on God's authority and he is under the Lord's influence. So justice and faithfulness are the marks by which one can recognise him.

3. Isaiah 11:6-9 portrays the *kingdom of peace as consequence of the new ruler's influence*. It appears as the purpose of his reign. Peace is described as manifesting itself between one animal and another as well as between human beings and animals. The effects of his rule are not limited to the world of humankind, but are also extended to the whole world of nature. However, it should be observed that the picture of peace among the animals does not represent an idyllic marginal note to a political programme, but rather important elements of this programme. And, it must be noted, these elements are peculiar to the role and relationships of each animal. The lamb offers hospitality to the wolf and the leopard finds a place to sleep beside the kid. Wild animals become friends

with tame animals, and both together are led by a child. This images show not only a peaceful harmony among the animals, or between human beings and animals, but also *the reversal of relationships between the strong and the weak.* This reversal, a contrast to our situation today, is also seen in the play of the suckling and the weaned child with the serpents and in the lion which eats straw like cattle. There are links here to the story of creation in Genesis 1-2, in which human beings and animals are partners with one another. The rule of humankind over the earth and the animals is carried out without bloodshed. Both human beings and animals are offered only vegetable nourishment (Gen. 1:29). So the images in verses 6-8 (cf. also Isa. 65:25 and Hos. 2:18) *of an end to devouring and being devoured* call forth in us a desire to return to the world of Paradise. Thus the kingdom of peace is realised, not in that we no longer have enemies, but rather that the enmity between completely different groups of creatures is ended. The solution is not the elimination of all the wild animals, but rather the hoped-for peace comes through deliberate implementation. Therefore we no longer do evil, and no longer experience it, on the Lord's holy mountain. This is the sign that the knowledge of the Lord has been fulfilled.

Question 3: Purpose (What is expected of us?)

The coming ruler is shown to be the one who guarantees justice, shown clearly by his inclination towards the least powerful creatures. A kingdom of peace among the animals, and between them and human beings, is portrayed as a manifestation of this justice. Peace requires that there be justice, and justice is oriented to peace. But the decisive point is *how* this kingdom of peace comes about. Peace comes not through the destruction of all enemies, but through *ending the enmity.* It is especially the transformation of the wild animals (which are the strong ones) which is the pre-condition for the kingdom of peace. The basic motives and the guiding intentions of the kingdom of peace have social and political dimensions. The question as to whether this expectation can be realised does not seem to be under consideration here. The text does not ask whether the lion will really eat straw like the ox, but rather *what is the constellation* between the strong and the weak in which the kingdom of peace will manifest itself, and *what is the practice for today* which is appropriate to this hope for peace. Indeed, the indicative mood of the promise must be turned into the imperative mood of decision-making.

Ezekiel 36:24-28

Question 4: Introduction (what is this text about?)

Because of its impurity, Israel had to be driven out of its land. But the fact of Israel's being driven out caused the name of God to be desecrated among the nations. Now the Lord decides, for the sake of the Lord's own honour, to bring Israel back home. The Lord grants the Israelites a new future, even though they have not deserved it.

Question 5: Prayer (how can a new future begin?)

A new future begins with the renewal of a people, with the granting of a permanent right to remain in the land. The renewal takes place in three phases. 1) The first phase is cleansing from all impurity. The Lord's cleansing action is illustrated as being like a ritual act by the priest (Lev. 14:49-53; cf. also Num. 19). Through being sprinkled with water, each individual among the people is to be cleansed of all impurity. 2) The second phase is the gift of a new heart and a new spirit. The new heart is described as a heart of flesh, in contrast to a heart of stone. The hearts of the people, which have become hardened, are changed by the Lord's act into new hearts, which are willing to hear and to learn the commandments of God. 3) The third phase is the pouring out of the Lord's Spirit. This completes the renewal of the people. The Spirit of God is one of *renewing power and life-creating might* (cf. 1 Sam. 10:6-7; Isa. 32:15). It leads a person to be united with the will and the nature of God. The Spirit of the Lord is poured into the person's heart, so that the person will obey the Lord. But not through this one-time event, but rather *because the spirit remains* will human life be shaped according to God's commandments (cf. Isa. 11:2). This is what makes true communion possible between God and human being, as stated in the covenant. So this is how we should pray for a new future: *Come, Holy Spirit. Renew us!*

Instructions for Bible study

This Bible study should be built around the questions in parentheses. The leader can ask each question, and clarify the answer for each paragraph in dialogue with the participants. After Question 5, the Bible study ends with a prayer for the pouring out of the spirit, for a new beginning for each individual or for the group.

Ezekiel 36:22-28   J. Prior

S̲ay to the House of Israel, "The Lord God says this: I am acting not for your sake, House of Israel, but for the sake of my holy name, which you have profaned among the nations where you have gone. I am going to display the holiness of my great name, which has been profaned among the nations, which you have profaned among them. And the nations will know that I am the Lord – declares the Lord God – when in you I display my holiness before their eyes. For I shall take you from among the nations and gather you back from all the countries, and bring you home to your own country. I shall pour clean water over you and you will be cleansed; I shall cleanse you of all your filth and of all your foul idols. I shall give you a new heart, and put a new spirit in you; I shall remove the heart of stone from your bodies and give you a heart of flesh instead. I shall put my spirit in you, and make you keep my laws, and respect and practise my judgments. You will live in the country which I gave your ancestors. You will be my people and I shall be your God."

At long last, following chapter after chapter of relentless challenge and accusation, following diatribe after diatribe against ritual sacrilege and social profanation, the prophet utters a quiet word of hope. Finally, after harsh indictment and stark symbol, Ezekiel is enlightened by a salvific glow.

Ezekiel is the first prophet to speak from exile, from outside the Promised Land, from Babylon, capital of the colonial empire. His voice is heard for some 22 years (BCE 593-571). From bitter banishment, he grapples with God's apparent failure. Who can respect a god who cannot even protect the god's own people on their own land? The three pillars of the Torah have evidently collapsed: the pledge of land to ensure fecundity, the security of a Davidic dynasty to guarantee justice, the promise of a temple and priesthood to proclaim God's Word authentically.

The prophecy of Ezekiel is not for the faint-hearted, for those who look for an instant salvific solution before courageously facing utter catastrophe. For the world of Ezekiel is a world in chaos; the empire has seemingly won while God's people is fast assimilating itself to occupation at home and settling down to marginalization in exile. God's people have proved fickle and faithless, swiftly embracing the dominant values of the empire, the idols of cultic, military and political might. The social fabric is crumbling, for greed and violence are as infectious as they are numbing. The poor are ignored and God's holiness profaned among the nations. In times like these, Ezekiel has little time for the tenderness of an Isaiah or the encouragement of an evangelist.

And yet, when death has seemingly won at home and abroad, the prophet resists every attempt to be "normalized", to conform, to be assimilated into the world around him. If it is true that "only dead fish follow the current", there would seem to be little evidence of life among the exiles in Babylon. Yet as long as the prophet's faith is alive, he will not grow spiritually numb.

And yes, the prophet finally sees that we are not beyond redemption, that the political, religious and ecological mess we have made of God's world may indeed be healed. Dawn is breaking for those who have squarely faced the long darkness. Long delayed, these are words of renewal and restoration: a new people with a new spirit return to their ancestral land and rebuild Jerusalem (Ezekiel 40-48). Renovation is to be carried out under a renewed leadership in the hands of shepherds after God's own heart (Ezek. 34).

In Ezekiel 36:22-32 we read the core of Ezekiel's theology of salvation: the "failed" god of 12 minor tribes is none other than the universal God of the nations. God, witness to our wrongdoing, is giving this people a new heart and a new spirit. A transformed humanity will channel God's holiness and witness to God's glory among the nations. God's glorious name is being revealed in a new leadership for a renewed people who are being reinstated in their ancestral lands. Sola gratia, salvation solely through God's initiative and God's grace; sola fide, a people cleansed from ritual pollution and social stain in God's clean water.

The human heart is the centre of personality, the source of every thought, the fountain of the will. Gone is the insensitive, preoccupied and grasping heart of stone, replaced by a responsive heart of flesh, a heart fully awake and wholly aware. Gone is the numbing assimilated spirit, replaced by a life force that truly moves and motivates, directing intentions, thoughts and attitudes. The presence of God's Spirit within transforms motivation; only then are we capable of living according to God's Word.

Not for Ezekiel a planting of God's law within our present heart (as against Jeremiah 31:31-34), but rather a total heart replacement and an utterly new spirit. With new heart and new spirit the people can look at life from God's own viewpoint and live as a community rather than as scattered individuals. This is the sign of a new age, the age of the Messiah (see Ezek. 37:14, 39:29, Joel 2:28-29) when "You will be my people and I shall be your God". This key covenant formula is found elsewhere in Ezekiel (Ezek. 14:11; 37:23, 27), in other prophetic writings (Jer. 7:23, 11:4, 24:7, 31:33, Hos. 2:23, Zech. 8:8) and in the Torah itself (Ex. 6:7).

The new heart and new spirit heal the people from loss of hope due to the apparent loss of God's promises (land, kingship, temple). The people are restored to a new sense of mission and once again become a channel to the nations flowing with God's holiness.

Having apparently lost everything, a small, prophetically-inspired group of exiles later showed themselves at their most creative: they compiled the Hebrew Bible. This written scripture, produced in exile, has proved more secure than any homeland, more permanent than political kingship, and has opened more hearts to God's Word than any quantity of temple sacrifice.

Personal/group reflection and study

Prayerful reflection in three steps

1. Read through the passage slowly. Remain silent for a while until a particular word or phrase stands out. In a group each person is given an opportunity to say aloud the word or phrase that is most striking to the reader. More than one person may have chosen the same phrase.

2. Read through the passage slowly again. Remain silent for awhile, and then each person who wishes may briefly mention why that particular word or phrase is striking. No long sermon, just a simple sharing.

3. Read through the passage slowly once more. Remain silent for awhile, and then each person who wishes may turn the phrase they have chosen into a short prayer.

Study in context

One or more of the following themes may be shared and discussed.

Assimilation

What values of the surrounding culture have been assimilated by your Christian community? What numbing influence does assimilation bring?

What biblical values stand out in stark contrast to those of contemporary society?

Do you feel closer to Ezekiel's small community bravely living a "contrast culture", or to the larger Hebrew community that had already assimilated itself to Babylonian society?

Assimilation brings numbing indifference and gives scope to shallow personal ambition. What changes need to take place in order for our intentions, thoughts and attitudes to be attuned to God's Word?

Witness to God's holiness

Share your experience of God's grandeur. What impact does God's greatness have on your daily life?

Give examples of how God's holiness has pierced the shallow, consumer culture of the global market or softened the crass, violent culture of domination.

New heart, new spirit

Share inspiring examples of someone who has become a "completely new person" and left behind the values of wealth and power, and now witnesses to the God of compassionate justice and truthful love.

Healing

The repressive Babylonian state brought about harmony through coercion. Oppression and exploitation preserved the status quo. In these unpromising conditions a minority group of exiled Hebrews creatively produced a written scripture. The "People of the Book" rose again in hope, with a new sense of mission.

However unpromising our present day situation, how could a new heart – fully awake and wholly aware – give us a new sense of mission, a mission of healing and reconciliation?

Luke 4:14-21   J. Prior

---

*J*esus, *with the power of the Spirit in him, returned to Galilee; and
his reputation spread throughout the countryside. He taught in
their synagogues and everyone glorified him. He came to Nazareth,
where he had been brought up, and went into the synagogue on the
Sabbath day as he usually did. He stood up to read, and they
handed him the scroll of the prophet Isaiah. Unrolling the scroll he
found the place where it is written: The spirit of the Lord is on me,
for he has anointed me to bring the good news to the afflicted. He
has sent me to proclaim liberty to captives, sight to the blind, to let
the oppressed go free, to proclaim a year of favour from the Lord.
Then he rolled up the scroll, gave it back to the assistant and sat
down. And all eyes in the synagogue were fixed on him. Then he
began to speak to them, "This text is being fulfilled today even while
you are listening."*

Reflection

With the power of the Spirit, Jesus taught in Galilean synagogues and then came to obscure and tiny Nazareth (see John
1:16) to worship as was his custom. There each Sabbath the community sang a psalm, recited the Shema (Deut. 6:4-5) and the 18
Benedictions, read from the Torah (Law) and then from the
Prophets, heard a sermon on the meaning of the readings,
received a blessing by the president and concluded with the
priestly blessing of Nb 6:24-27.

We are not sure whether there was a cycle of readings in first
century Palestine. If there was, then the scroll handed to Jesus
would be open at Isaiah 61 with a marker at the verse to be read.
If not, then Jesus chose the reading himself, unrolling the scroll

16

almost to the end. He read Isaiah 61:1-2 replacing one phrase and leaving out much of the final verse. Maybe this was the version of the Aramaic Scriptures used in Galilee at the time; if not, then Jesus himself made the changes. And so the text quoted by Jesus (Luke 4:16-18) is woven from Isaiah 61:1-2 and Isaiah 58:6. Jesus omits those elements that might either spiritualize the text (*"to heal the broken hearted"*) or threaten his audience (*"to announce a day of vengeance"*). He then sharpens the whole by inserting the phrase, *"to let the oppressed go free."* The text thus becomes clearly focused as glad tidings to the oppressed. Jesus is a sharply focused person.

In all probability *"the afflicted"*, *"the captives"* and *"the blind"* refer to the same oppressed group, namely the poorest of the poor who are in prison due to debt. The term "poor" is not to be interpreted metaphorically. The poor are those who are economically and socially oppressed. Prisoners were blinded because underground prisons were bereft of sunlight. The poor are placed at the centre of the gospel because they are the least, the lowliest, the lost.

Jesus announces a "Jubilee", a forgiveness of debt. We recall Luke's version of the Lord's Prayer, *"Forgive us our debts for we ourselves forgive each one who is in debt to us."* (Luke 11:3). The biblical Jubilee was held each 50 years when fields lay fallow, families returned to their ancestral homelands, debts were cancelled and slaves set free. The Jubilee restored a rough equality between and clans. The inevitable increase in inequality and injustice over the years must be levelled down each half-century. Faith in a sovereign God should be mirrored in the structures of social and economic life which, in turn, ought to echo the pattern of God's realm. The community could start afresh. Such Jubilee reflections have been uncovered at Qumran, site of a first century Jewish movement. In Qumran the text used by Jesus from Isaiah 61 was linked to the Jubilee texts of Leviticus 25:10-13 and Deuteronomy 15:2.

Jesus slipped in the phrase *"let the oppressed go free"* from Isaiah 58:6. In Hebrew the oppressed are the "downtrodden", those broken in pieces, the oppressed in spirit. In India today they are known as the Dalits – the "broken ones".

By quoting Isaiah, Jesus claims that he is both a messianic prophet of the sort that Samaria awaited, and a messianic king of the kind that Judea expected, one capable of setting in motion the wondrous events envisioned by Isaiah.

This word of Jesus is proclaimed *"in the power of the Spirit"*. This is Jesus' inaugural sermon when he outlines the programme for his whole life and ministry. This "charter sermon" encapsulates the gospel in miniature. This is what Jesus is about. Here we find the direction and scope of his mission that will find its fulfilment in death and resurrection. This first sermon declares Jesus' preference for the afflicted, the captives, the blind and the oppressed. At the opening of his public ministry Jesus is presented as the one who has a clear, personal preference for a certain group who can place its hope in him because the acceptable time of favour has come for all the forgotten people. This is the key in understanding the rest of the gospel.

The text presents Jesus as a "teacher" (Luke 4:5). This is a pervasive theme in Luke where Jesus is called "teacher" some thirteen times. The teacher's way is normative for his disciples.

Jesus' mission is addressed to all nations (Luke 4:25-27); he shares neither the small-mindedness nor the niggardly vision of his Nazareth congregation. Jesus stands outside their pettiness. He does not share their clannish idea of salvation, their mean image of God or their suspicious view of each other.

Jesus' concern is a universal concern for the underprivileged and the outcast, a statement of commitment to social justice and reform, fostering outreach to all in peace. This is spelt out in more detail in the "Sermon on the Plain" (Luke 6:20-49).

Today this Scripture is being fulfilled (Luke 4:21). *"Today"* – the fulfilment is already present.

The congregation reacts in a variety of ways: with enthusiasm (Luke 4:15), admiration (Luke 4:22), doubt (Luke 4:23), small-mindedness (Luke 4:23) and, finally, with anger (Luke 4:28).

Personal/group reflection and study

Prayerful reflection in three steps

1. Read through the passage slowly. Remain silent for a while until a particular word or phrase stands out. In a group each person is given an opportunity to say aloud the word or phrase that is most striking to the reader. More than one person may have chosen the same phrase.

2. Read through the passage slowly again. Remain silent for awhile, and then each person who wishes may briefly mention why that particular word or phrase is striking. No long sermon, just a simple sharing.

3. Read through the passage slowly once more. Remain silent for awhile, and then each person who wishes may turn the phrase they have chosen into a short prayer.

Study in context

One or more of the following themes may be shared/studied.

The poor

Who are the poorest of the poor, the least, the lowliest, the lost?

Do we listen to them?

How do we acknowledge them, accept them, embrace them, stand at their side?

How do we place the poor at the centre of the gospel of liberty, at the heart of our Christian community life and worship, as the recipients of the Lord's year of favour? Do we see the poor more as objects of our concern or as witnesses of the Lord's Jubilee? ➤

Debt

Share information on the slavery of debt today – both those in debt in your neighbourhood and overseas. What have we been doing to free the poor of crippling debt – charity, awareness-building, advocacy, simplifying lifestyle?

Having shared information and activity to date, reread Luke 4:14-21. What new insights do we gain?

Inaugural text

You have been handed the scroll of the scriptures. You wish to read a short passage that sums up who you are, what values your life is witness to, what (whom) you live and are ready to die for. You wish to speak simply, sincerely, without any pretensions. What passage do you choose, and why?

What are the honest reactions of the other members of the group?

John 4:5-30 John C. Thomas

So he came to a Samaritan city called Sychar, near the plot of ground that Jacob had given to his son Joseph. Jacob's well was there, and Jesus, tired out by his journey, was sitting by the well. It was about noon.

A Samaritan woman came to draw water, and Jesus said to her, "Give me a drink." (His disciples had gone to the city to buy food.) The Samaritan woman said to him, "How is it that you, a Jew, ask a drink of me, a woman of Samaria?" (Jews do not share things in common with Samaritans.) Jesus answered her, "If you knew the gift of God, and who it is that is saying to you, 'Give me a drink', you would have asked him, and he would have given you living water." The woman said to him, "Sir, you have no bucket, and the well is deep. Where do you get that living water? Are you greater than our ancestor Jacob, who gave us the well, and with his sons and his flocks drank from it?"

Jesus said to her, "Everyone who drinks of this water will be thirsty again, but those who drink of the water that I will give them will never be thirsty. The water that I will give will become in them a spring of water gushing up to eternal life." The woman said to him, "Sir, give me this water, so that I may never be thirsty or have to keep coming here to draw water." Jesus said to her, "Go, call your husband, and come back." The woman answered him, "I have no husband." Jesus said to her, "You are right in saying, 'I have no husband'; for you have had five husbands, and the one you have now is not your husband. What you have said is true!" The woman said to him, "Sir, I see that you are a prophet. Our ancestors worshipped on this mountain, but you say that the place where people must worship is in Jerusalem." Jesus said to her, "Woman, believe me, the hour is coming when you will worship the Father neither on this

mountain nor in Jerusalem. You worship what you do not know; we worship what we know, for salvation is from the Jews. But the hour is coming, and is now here, when the true worshippers will worship the Father in spirit and truth, for the Father seeks such as these to worship him. God is spirit, and those who worship him must worship in spirit and truth." The woman said to him, "I know that Messiah is coming" (who is called Christ). "When he comes, he will proclaim all things to us." Jesus said to her, "I am he, the one who is speaking to you."
Just then his disciples came. They were astonished that he was speaking with a woman, but no one said, "What do you want?" or, "Why are you speaking with her?" Then the woman left her water jar and went back to the city. She said to the people, "Come and see a man who told me everything I have ever done! He cannot be the Messiah, can he?" They left the city and were on their way to him.

The role attributed to the Holy Spirit in the gospel according to John is distinctive amongst the canonical gospels. In this gospel, the work of the Spirit is intimately connected with the person and ministry of Jesus, for the first mention of the Spirit is in regard to Jesus' identity as the one upon whom the Spirit descends and remains upon (1:32-33). It comes as no surprise to the readers that it is the one upon whom the Spirit descends who is identified as the one who will baptize with the Holy Spirit.

Near the beginning of this gospel, the readers discover that those who believe are given authority to become children of God, to be born of God (1:12-13). Later it is learned that the Spirit is the means by which believers experience "birth from above", for it is necessary to be born of water and Spirit to see the Kingdom of God (3:5). Though the work of the Spirit is like the wind, being sometimes difficult to determine where it comes from and where it goes (3:8), those born of the Spirit are able to discern his activity.

In his conversation with the Samaritan woman, Jesus uses the term "living/running water" in reference to the Spirit. While this woman thinks Jesus is referring to an underground stream of "running" water, he is actually inviting her to tap into the "living water" that he makes available to her. For the water of which he speaks will quench her thirst forever and will be a well of water leaping up into eternal life. The dynamic nature of the Spirit's activity is conveyed in part by the fact that the words "leaping up" are normally used to describe the activity of animals or humans, not inanimate objects like water. But when the believer taps into this underground river, it becomes a dynamic well in them. It is by means of the Spirit and the Truth (Jesus) that worship of the Father is possible and indeed necessary (4:23), for God is Spirit and he must be worshipped in Spirit and Truth (4:24).

In John 6:63 the readers learn that there is an extremely tight interplay between "eating the flesh" and "drinking his blood" and the work of the Spirit.

The Spirit's work is further elucidated in John 7:37-39. Though the text says that "the Spirit was not yet", it is clear that the believers know the Spirit's activity in the ministry of Jesus and the lives of those who believe in him. The words of 7:39 indicate that it is "out of his belly" that "rivers of living water" will flow. This language builds on the words directed to the Samaritan woman, identifying Jesus as the source of the living water that will spring forth from the well located in the believer. The appearance of the plural, "rivers", may indicate that in addition to experiencing birth from above, there may be other experiences of the Spirit in store for the believers.

In John 14-16, the future role for and additional experiences of the Spirit are indeed described by Jesus. The Spirit, who comes from the Father at Jesus' own request (14:16), is called another Paraclete, indicating that he is to function like Jesus. He is the Spirit of Truth (14:17), underscoring the intricate connection between Jesus, who is the Truth (14:6), and the Spirit who speaks on his behalf, the Spirit of Truth. Like Jesus, the Spirit is not received by the world but by believers, who know him (14:17). The Spirit will teach the disciples all things and remind them of the things which Jesus said (14:26). He will inspire their witness in the world (15:26-27) and convict the world of "sin, righteousness and judgment" (16:8-11).

The gospel concludes with two proleptic promises of the Spirit. When Jesus dies upon the cross (19:30), the Greek text says that he "gave the S/spirit", a phrase which could possibly mean that he expired, but perhaps conveys the idea that the gift of the Spirit is tied to his death. Later, when Jesus appears to the disciples after the resurrection he commands them to "receive the Holy Spirit" (20:22). This final promise and command with regard to the Spirit rings in the readers' ears as the gospel closes.

If the gospels are foundational documents for the various New Testament communities which they represent, what are the implications of the teaching of the gospel of John on the role of the Holy Spirit for contemporary Christians?

First, divine begetting, "birth from above", is possible only by means of the Spirit. This experience, that comes to those who believe, results in one becoming a child of God. Is this experience of the Spirit present in your life? If so, describe this event to a trusted brother or sister.

Second, the experience of the Spirit in the life of the believer is described as a dynamic one. In fact, Jesus uses the language of "a well of water leaping up unto eternal life". Identify an occasion when you felt the presence of the Spirit was leaping forth in your life.

Third, the Spirit's role in the life of the believer is perceived to be quite active, for he leads believers into all truth, reminds them of what Jesus said and convicts the world of sin, righteousness and judgment. In what ways have you sensed the active presence of the Spirit in your life and that of your community in any of these or other concrete ways?

Fourth, part of the Spirit's role is to inspire witness on behalf of Jesus' followers. Have you ever been conscious of such Spirit-inspired witness in your own life? When have you seen it in the lives of others? What was the result of such inspired witness?

Fifth, the repeated commands of Jesus with regard to the Spirit serve as a refrain calling us to receive all the Spirit has for disciples of Jesus. What impact does such a refrain have upon your own spiritual life? Is there more of the Spirit that you need? Exactly what do you need? How do you plan to respond to this lack?

2 Called in Christ to Be Reconciling and Healing Communities

Romans 10:17 and 12:1-21
Konstantin Nikolakopoulos

So faith comes from what is heard, and what is heard come through the word of Christ.

I appeal to you therefore, brothers and sisters, by the mercies of God, to present your bodies as a living sacrifice, holy and acceptable to God, which is your spiritual worship. Do not be conformed to this world, but be transformed by the renewing of your minds, so that you may discern what is the will of God – what is good and acceptable and perfect. For by the grace given to me I say to everyone among you not to think of yourself more highly than you ought to think, but to think with sober judgment, each according to the measure of faith that God has assigned. For as in one body we have many members, and not all the members have the same function, so we, who are many, are one body in Christ, and individually we are members one of another. We have gifts that differ according to the grace given to us: prophecy, in proportion to faith; ministry, in ministering; the teacher, in teaching; the exhorter, in exhortation; the giver, in generosity; the leader, in diligence; the compassionate, in cheerfulness. Let love be genuine; hate what is evil, hold fast to what is good; love one another with mutual affection; outdo one another in showing honour. Do not lag in zeal, be ardent in spirit, serve the Lord. Rejoice in hope, be patient in suffering, persevere in prayer. Contribute to the needs of the saints; extend hospitality to strangers. Bless those who persecute you; bless and do not curse them. Rejoice with those who rejoice, weep with those who weep. Live in harmony with one another; do not be haughty, but associate with the lowly; do not claim to be wiser than you are. Do not repay anyone evil for evil, but take thought for what is noble in the sight of all. It if is possible, so far as it depends on youl live peaceably with all. Beloved, never avenge yourselves, but leave room for the wrath of God; for it is written, "Vengeance is mine, I will repay, says the Lord." No, "if your enemies are hungry, feed them; if they are thirsty, give them something to drink; for by doing this you will heap burning coals on their heads." Do not be overcome by evil, but overcome evil with good.

The theme

The faith which comes from listening to this message and taking it to heart strengthens fellowship and mutual solidarity within the congregation and further afield.

Interpretation and reflection

Through his well known letter to the Romans Paul addresses two groups within the Roman congregation of that time: the Jewish Christians and the Gentile Christians. Through his highly developed theological arguments he highlighted the most important source of Christian experience for both groups: the Word of God as it is heard (Rom. 10:17), the proclamation, the kerygma. It does not matter whether the privileged Jewish Christians have inherited the basic foundations of their faith through their forbears and the prophets or whether the Gentile Christians have experienced faith through later evangelisation, for both groups it is through the proclamation of the word that they have learnt of and experienced faith which saves.

It is true that in the first instance the source and mainspring of faith is the word that is heard, the proclamation, however the word alone does not suffice to bring about salvation. On the one hand the word that is heard, called by Paul, "the word of Christ", demonstrates the invitation of Jesus Christ or his call to every human being. Faced with this call Jewish Christians and Gentile Christians – and in our modern society all people – are equal. Paul underlines this truth in crystal clear terms "For there is no distinction between Jew and Greek; the same Lord is Lord of all and is generous to all who call on him" (Rom. 10:12). On the other hand the human response to this proclamation is of enormous importance. Paul calls this response people make "obedience" and makes a direct link with eschatological salvation (Rom. 10:16). One must give oneself up in obedience to the Gospel, to become part of the Church which makes up the body of Christ (Rom. 12:5).

The immediate consequences of consciously lived out faith are mirrored in the life of the congregation. In Orthodox ecclesiology the congregation is the most lively cell of what we refer to as the Church. This is the beautiful biblical image that Paul offers us in Romans chapter 12, "For as in one body we have many members, and not all the members have the same function, so we, who are many, are one body in Christ, and individually we are members one of another" (Rom. 12:4-5).

Through the word (the proclamation) that is heard in Jesus Christ we are called to follow and serve him. It is precisely through this calling (in Greek: ek-kalein) that we Christians get to the substance of the Church (in Greek: Ek-klesia). The call, the invitation of our Lord also continues within the Church, within the congregation. Romans chapter 12 impresses upon us the interrelation between the kerygma and the function of the congregation in a way which is a continuations of the issues dealt with in chapter 10. This part has the clear characteristic of an paraenese (exhortation) or paraclesis, which depends upon the word that is heard and demonstrates the consequences of faith in this kerygmatic word.

In Pauline congregational theology every member plays an important role. Every Christian can, according to their talents and abilities, offer their particular services to the life of the congregation or community (Rom. 12:6-8), which presupposes that everyone will "be transformed by the renewing of your minds" (Rom. 12:2). People's spiritual metamorphosis which Paul both reminds us about and encourages us towards should always have as a goal "that you may discern what is the will of God — what is good and acceptable and perfect".

After the first 8 verses of chapter 12, which outline the spiritual directions of the following exhortations and which serve as both an introduction and a form of conclusion to the whole chapter, Paul concentrates on an analytical description of the congregational life he seeks. Although the whole of the passage Romans 12:9-21 makes up a beautiful mosaic of virtuous exhortations, the requirements of agape (love) are unmistakable from the very beginning. Verse 9a could even serve as the title for the whole of the following passage "Let love be genuine."

The essential features of Christian congregational life are clearly set out in the 12:9-21 passage. Paul offers us a series of practical exhortations which are not only valid for the congregation in Rome but which are of timeless value. To practice love one must reactivate various other virtues as well, such as mutual affection, showing honour (12:10), hope, patience, prayer (12:12), hospitality (12:13), blessing and goodness (12:14), mutual assistance (12:15), harmony and no haughty feelings (12:16), not repaying evil and taking revenge, but seeking peace and reconciliation (12:17-21).

It is of course significant that in part the exhortations of the letter to the Romans address the situation within the congregation and in part they address the relationship of the congregation with non-Christians. The Apostle exhorts Christians to make bodily offerings of themselves, in other words, to be a holy and living sacrifice, pleasing to God and resulting in putting this spiritual transformation into practice for one neighbour. Human relations need continual salvation and lasting reconciliation. And these two great visions (salvation and reconciliation) should from a Christian point of view, regard both we Christians amongst ourselves and also our non-Christian fellow human beings as the final recipients. Over the centuries relations between Christians have deteriorated leading to so many divisions, this needs the antidote of salvation and reconciliation. But after restoring the shattered image of ecumenical Christianity then all Christians need to be concerned about reconciliation and healing their relationships with all citizens of this planet who have not necessarily accepted the Christian message.

Methodological material

1. **The following issues for discussion could be dealt with in groups:**
   - What is the theological and sociological significance of the concept of "Church"
   - The heavenly church (triumphant) and the earthy members (struggling)
   - What should the organization of a Christian congregation be?
   - To whom do we address Christian evangelization today?
   - Where should we engage in Mission and where in evangelization or neo-evangelization?

➤

- A reflection on the differences within Christianity and the discovery of the attitudes of various groups that hinder ecumenism.
- How is Christian obedience to be understood and practised?
- Spiritual father - obedience - Orthodox spiritual life
- The theological basis and significance of the saving of each human being from an Orthodox perspective
- Symbiosis within the congregation (The application of the virtues that have been mentioned in various situations)
- The relationship of Christians to non-Christians

2. **The following current situations could be discussed in a group:**
- The Orthodox and Roman Catholic version of Christianity
- Orthodox Greece and its small Protestant minority
- New developments in western European Christianity: the recent arrival of Orthodoxy in the 20th century
- Ancient traumas – new attempts at healing: church schism (1054), the fourth crusade (1204)
- The centuries-old coexistence of Orthodox and Jews (e.g. in Greece)
- Orthodox traditions in a Muslim country: the Ecumenical Patriarchate of Constantinople in Turkish Istanbul
- Reconciled coexistence between the three great monotheistic traditions

3. **The following illustrations might be helpful**
- The encounter of a committed Christian with a well-intentioned heathen (illustrated example: Acts 8:26-39)
- The situation of a Christian before they have confessed – the need for reconciliation with ones enemies (illustrated example: Matthew 5:23-26)

Luke 15:11-32   H. Pappas

---

*T*hen Jesus said, "There was a man who had two sons. The younger of them said to his father, 'Father, give me the share of the property that will belong to me.' So he divided his property between them. A few days later the younger son gathered all he had and traveled to a distant country, and there he squandered his property in dissolute living. When he had spent everything, a severe famine took place throughout that country, and he began to be in need. So he went and hired himself out to one of the citizens of that country, who sent him to his fields to feed the pigs. He would gladly have filled himself with the pods that the pigs were eating; and no one gave him anything. But when he came to himself he said, 'How many of my father's hired hands have bread enough and to spare, but here I am dying of hunger! I will get up and go to my father, and I will say to him, "Father, I have sinned against heaven and before you, I am no longer worthy to be called your son; treat me like one of your hired hands." So he set off and went to his father. But while he was still far off, his father saw him and was filled with compassion; he ran and put his arms around him and kissed him. Then the son said to him, 'Father, I have sinned against heaven and before you; I am no longer worthy to be called your son.' But the father said to his slaves, 'Quickly, bring out a robe – the best one – and put it on him; put a ring on his finger and sandals on his feet. And get the fatted calf and kill it, and let us eat and celebrate; for this son of mine was dead and is alive again; he was lost and is found!' And they began to celebrate. "Now his elder son was in the field; and when he came and approached the house, he heard music and dancing. He called one of the slaves and asked what was going on. He replied, 'Your brother has come, and your father has killed the fatted calf, because he has got him back safe and sound. Then *he became angry and refused to go in. His father came out and begin to plead with him. But he answered his father 'Listen! For all these years I have been working like a slave for you, and I have never disobeyed your command; yet you have never given me even a young goat so that I might celebrate with my friends. But when this son of yours came back, who has devoured your property with prostitutes, you killed the fatted calf for him. Then the father said to him, 'Son, you are always with me, and all that is mine is yours. But we had to celebrate and rejoice, because this brother of yours was dead and has come to life; he was lost and has been found.'"*

Luke 15:1-2: To his contemporary fellow Jews, Jesus Christ often attracted a strange crowd – government conspirators who overcharged fellow citizens for their own benefit (tax collectors), immoral people and unobservant believers (sinners). Moreover, he openly shared meals with them, leaving himself open to charges of ritual uncleanness.

The religious leadership of the day (Pharisees and scribes), often depicted in the four gospels as hardened in self-righteousness, complained about Jesus' behaviour and actions.[1] In particular, they accused Jesus of grossly violating the rules for table fellowship, carefully regulated by Jewish tradition.

In Luke 15, Jesus responds by telling three parables that illustrate saving truths about the radical nature of the kingdom of God. All three involve "lost and found" themes. All three reveal God's abundant joy and gracious acceptance of any sinner who repents (15:7). The third, and longest, is about one lost son out of two – though the other, it turns out, is in peril even though he never physically left the father (15:11-32).

The lost son, the loving father and the elder brother

Stories about families are deeply embedded in the Bible, beginning with the first book, Genesis. In the ancient world, the first born son was normally entitled to receive a double portion of inheritance from the father, and was considered most important of all the children. However, the stories in Genesis reveal that a younger son often is the one through whom God works, overturning what is expected in human society: Cain slays Abel, Jacob bests Esau, Joseph saves his family.

In this parable, Jesus begins by saying that there are two sons of one father (v. 11). The younger asks for and receives his full inheritance from the father (v. 12). Such a request expresses the attitude that the parent is as good as dead, since the child cannot wait for the parent to die. Indeed, in cultures that still practice such customs, it is absolutely unthinkable that any child would ever do this.[2] Thus, Jesus is describing a family scene that is shocking and without precedent. Even the behaviour of the father is unlike any human parent: immediate compliance, with no questions asked and no conditions stipulated.[3]

Soon afterwards, the younger brother, loaded with money, leaves for a distant place (no doubt gentile territory) where he squanders everything in reckless, immoral living (v. 13). When all has been spent, he finds himself afflicted not only by poverty but by famine (v. 14). This was something that everyone feared in the ancient world where the ability to grow crops and maintain livestock was not as regulated or protected as in developed countries today. Famine in the Bible often involves a spiritual crisis. Abraham, and later Jacob and his sons, had to abandon the land of God's promise and risk everything by traveling to a foreign place (Egypt) just to stay alive. Much later, Ruth and Naomi were forced to do the same in going to Moab. In this story, the younger son has become destitute not just physically but spiritually.

Once he realizes his own need, out of desperation, the younger son hires himself out to a wealthy citizen who assigns him the task of tending pigs (v. 15). The humiliation of working for a gentile is made worse since pigs were "unclean" animals in the eyes of Jewish dietary law. The younger son could easily have come to loathe himself in such a degraded and shameful job. He even yearns for the pig food itself, but tragically there is no one to help him (v. 16).

Finally, though, the younger brother "came to himself,"[4] and remembered his father's house (v. 17). This is the turning point in the first part of the story, reflecting both authentic self-awareness and memory. Next he resolves to get up,[5] go back home to his father,[6] confess his sin and unworthiness, and ask to be received as a hired laborer (vv. 17-19). Even if self-interest is involved, he is clearly willing to acknowledge his sin and has the humility to admit that he has forfeited his sonship.

The younger son starts his journey home. But before he is even close, his father *sees him, is moved by compassion, and runs to welcome him with open arms and a kiss* (v. 20). Unlike the first two "lost and found" stories in Luke 15, there is no active, outward searching for the lost in this story. Yet the father is anything but passive, for he surely has not been idling away his time, scorning his rebellious son or just "moving on with life". In fact, Jesus describes a father who never forgets a lost child, never loses hope, never hardens his heart, no matter how badly the child has behaved. And the homecoming is stunning: the father interrupts the son's confession (v. 22), orders the slaves to brings the symbols of honor (the best robe), inheritance (the ring and the sandals), and commands that the community (the extended household) gather in festive celebration with the choicest food (the fatted calf; v. 23). In conclusion, the father exclaims his motive: *for this son of mine was dead and is alive again; he was lost and is found* (v. 24)! Once again Jesus makes clear the joy and celebration of heaven over one person who repents and turns towards God (15:7,10).

It would seem much happier if the story ended here, but it does not. The elder son never had left the father's house and remained obedient and hard-working. Now, after yet another long day in the fields, he comes home only to hear the music and dancing. Instead of approaching his father directly (whose side he claims never to have left!), he demands an explanation from a slave (v. 25-26). Upon learning what is really happening (v. 27), the elder son becomes angry and refuses to come home and join in the community's celebration (v. 28a). He prefers self-isolation, and his physical distance from both the father and the community is explicit. Once again the father takes the initiative (he does not wait for this son, either!), comes out and pleads[7] with him (v. 28b). However, this son's reaction is direct and strident. Disrespectfully ("Listen!"), he focuses only on himself (working as a slave for years) and attacks both the father (who is accused of ingratitude and injustice) and the younger brother (vv. 29-30). The elder son is not only estranged from his younger brother ("this son of yours"), he is also alienated from his father's love.

The final word, though, belongs to the father. In full freedom and integrity, he responds in loving-kindness to these harsh words, confirming both the elder son's identity as a son, along with his status as heir (v. 31). Then the father reasserts his fundamental motive, the common theme of all three parables in Luke 15: celebration and joy is fitting since your brother "was dead and has come to life... was lost and has been found" (v. 32). God's generosity is not always pleasing to us, nor does it always appear just. We hear nothing further of this story: what will the elder brother finally do?

Reflection and application

1. A teenage daughter, unlike her respectful and compliant siblings, gradually becomes more and more the "black sheep" of the family through cigarette smoking by age 13, illegal drug use by age 15, engaging in casual sex by age 17. Eventually, after one more disastrous screaming match with mother, she is kicked out of the house and the locks on all doors are changed. Are parents ever justified in disowning their children? How can the church community respond to fractured families?

2. Reflect on the ways you, and your community of faith, have lived like the younger son – outwardly rebellious, leaving for "distant lands". How have you acted like the elder son – outwardly compliant and obedient, yet given to self-righteousness and judging others? Have you ever acted like the loving father – unconditionally loving, never forgetting, patient towards all?

3. How much is our identity (as individuals and as communities) based more upon our own achievements and self-worth than on God's gracious and unmerited forgiveness, grace and love? How important is it for us to recognize the shattering truth of God's gift of forgiveness of sins through Jesus Christ?

4. How can Christian communities exhibit the reconciling and healing love and mercy of God as revealed in this parable – with pregnant teenagers, drug addicts, those with sexually transmitted diseases, and so on? How can we love those caught in sin while holding them accountable for repentance? Note that the awesome joy and acceptance of God for the repenting son far exceeded anything that he had expected.

5. When we admit our own foolishness, and call to mind our *true home in heaven* (through any authentic turning toward God), we are re-connected (re-membered) to God's love that includes the community of God. Ultimately, God is community in God's own self – in the Trinity of three persons in perfect communion –

➤

as well as in God's own reaching out to us, the church. Can families and church communities build positive and healthy memories with young and old alike so that, when human beings stray and get lost spiritually, they may remember the love and unconditional acceptance of God offered through the people of God?

NOTES

[1] This recalls the Hebrew people who complained bitterly, and unfairly, against Moses in the wilderness, when they preferred the security of slavery back in Egypt to the uncertainty of freedom (Ex. 16:2). The word in the Septuagint (the Old Testament in ancient Greek) is the same as the New Testament Greek word in Luke – *diagogguzw*.

[2] Noted by Henri Nouwen in *The Return of the Prodigal Son*.

[3] Completely against traditional, pious advice as illustrated in Sirach 33:20-21,24.

[4] Some scholars point out that this is a Semitic idiom (also reflected in ancient Greek and Latin) that means "when he realized how foolish he had been".

[5] The Greek word is anastaj, the same word used for resurrection *(anastasij)*.

[6] Repentance in the Old Testament is often termed "turning" or "return" in Hebrew *(shub)*.

[7] The Greek verb parakalew has a range of meaning that suggests the father is not just begging his son, but encouraging and inviting him graciously.

Exodus 15:22-27
& 35:20-29,
and Mark 14:3-9   Mercedes García Bachmann

---

*T*hen Moses ordered Israel to set out from the Red Sea, and they
went into the wilderness of Shur. They went three days in the wilderness and found no water. When they came to Marah, they could not
drink the water of Marah because it was bitter. That is why it was
called Marah. And the people complained against Moses, saying,
"what shall we d rink?" He cried out to the Lord; and the Lord
showed him a piece of wood; he threw it into the water, and the water
became sweet. There the Lord made for them a statute and an ordi-
nance and there he put them to the test. He said, "If you will listen
carefully to the voice of the Lord your God, and do what is right in
his sight, and give heed to his commandments and keep all his
statutes, I will not bring upon you any of the diseases that I brought
upon the Egyptians; for I am the Lord who heals you." Then they
came to Elim, where there were twelve springs of water and seventy
palm trees; and they camped there by the water. (Ex.15:22-27)
Then all the congregation of the Israelites withdrew from the presence of Moses. And they came, everyone whose heart was stirred,
and everyone whose spirit was willing, and brought the Lord's offering to be used for the tent of meeting, and for all its service, and for
the sacred vestments. So they came, both men and women; all who
were of a willing heart brought brooches and earrings and signet
rings and pendants, all sorts of gold objects, everyone bringing an
offering of gold to the Lord. And everyone who possessed blue or
purple or crimson yarn or fine linen or goats' hair or tanned rams'
skins or fine leather, brought them. Everyone who could make an
offering of sliver or bronze brought it as the Lord's offering; and
everyone who possessed acacia wood of any use in the work, brought
it. All the skilful women spun with their hands, and brought what
they had spun in blue and and purple and crimson yarns and fine

*linen; all the women whose hearts moved them to use their skill spun
the goats' hair. And the leaders brought onyx stones and gems to be
set in the ephod and the breastpiece, and spices and oil for the light,
and for the anointing oil, and for the fragrant incense. All the
Israelite men and women whose work that the Lord had commanded
by Moses to be done, brought it as a freewill offering to the Lord.
(Ex. 35:20-29)*

*While he was at Bethany in the house of Simon the leper, as he sat
at the table, a woman came with an alabaster jar of very costly ointment of nard, and she broke open the jar and poured the ointment
on his head. But some were there who said to one another in anger,
"Why was the ointment wasted in this way? For this ointment could
have been sold for more than three hundred denarii, and the money
given to the poor." And they scolded her. But Jesus said, "Let her
alone; why do you trouble her? She has performed a good service for
me. For you always have the poor with you, and you can show kindness to them whenever you wish; but you will not always have me.
She has done what she could; she has anointed my body beforehand
for its burial. Truly I tell you, wherever the good news is proclaimed
in the whole world, what she has done will be told in remembrance
of her." (Mark 14:3-9)*

This Bible study on three texts starts from the question: What
would be <u>one</u> element necessary for helping our communities to
become healing and reconciling agents in the world? In saying
"one element", I mean there may be several important elements,
but at least this one should not be overlooked.

I have chosen *tolerance of differences* as one necessary element
in building communities of healing and reconciliation. And about
this Bible study is about tolerance of differences.

"Tolerance" has a somewhat negative implication, as it means
less than whole-hearted acceptance of that in others which we do
not like or share. Yet at least tolerance implies recognition of differences and also recognition of elements in the other (the other
person, community, culture, country, continent, church, whatever) that we about which we are willing to talk and learn. We
also realize that others may need to be tolerant of us, in a variety
of ways. Rather than discriminate or ignore the other/s as of
lesser value than us, at least we should make an effort to tolerate
them, and eventually, to recognize their values and possibly come
to an acceptance of them.

This approach to tolerance could be a first, necessary step in
becoming healing, reconciling communities, as most of our world
rejects, persecutes, despises and even kills persons, peoples or

communities with whom they violently disagree. I propose some scriptural texts for study and several questions, so that Bible study groups consider a range of possibilities as bases for discussing tolerance, and choose the passage that addresses them most directly.

Introductory exercise

Think of your body; try to be more aware each part of it and how it feels. Do you feel your feet, your knees, your brows, your fingers, your bowels, your breast coming up and down with your breathing? Are you aware of your nails? Your skin? Your eyes? Is there any part of your body that you do not feel at this time or permanently? Have you suffered any kind of accident or illness that prevents you from feeling something somewhere?

Imagine now how the social body feels when "accidents" prevent us from being fully aware of certain members of the group or of society; when within the community we do not listen to, pay attention to, or otherwise "feel" certain members (notably children, youth, lesbians and gays, people with disabilities).

Optional question: What does it mean to be healing communities?

To me, it means to be communities where people and processes can be healthier, can get back to a more authentically united state of being, recover wholesomeness, harmony, well-being, *shalom.* I state this while recognizing that different cultures hold different views of what is "healthy" and what is not, and that societies vary in their approach to how people may be healed.

Question 1: Come together (as individuals, as Christian communities and as regional, ethnic or national communities) and honestly recognize that even if we are practicing Christians, we do not love our neighbours as ourselves; honestly recognize who are those neighbours we do not accept and which of their characteristics (real and stereotyped) we do not like; which are the ones we do like, which are the ones we fear or do not understand.

There are cultures in which health means to be rather weighty, have some fat in oneself; for others, to be healthy means to be extremely slim, live on a low-fat diet; for still others, health has more to do with low levels of stress than with food itself; and so forth. In the Bible, there aren't many definitions of health, nor of sickness, for that matter. There are a few instances, however, in which God's self-revelation to Israel is as a healer or physician, and Jesus' ministry was remarkably oriented towards healing the sick and expelling demons.[1]

Exodus 15:22-27

Read Exodus 15:22-27 in your Bibles. Pay particular attention to v. 26. Notice how the idea of health presented here has a strong, direct link to God's own action: "I am Yahweh your healer", which means, "No other power (human or divine) is your healer; only me."

The second important thing in this divine statement is that healing for Israel is bound together with listening to God's word and living it out: if you keep God's commandments and statutes, none of the plagues and sicknesses set upon Egypt will come upon you. This was realized as soon as the people had come out of bondage and had encountered their first difficulty in the dessert: unpotable water (Marah). Instead of waters of death as in Egypt with the plagues, these become waters of life. Yet, there is a condition: "If...".

Question 2: In your view, what are the conditions God puts on the people of God in order to achieve health and avoid sickness?

Israel is called to live as God's people and, through that call, to find wholeness and avoid sickness. Thus, in this text from Exodus 15, healing is linked to God's calling: God's people, gathered in diverse communities around the world, are called to the twin tasks of healing and reconciling.

Question 3: In your view, is there any difference between people who seek to live according to God's will within Christian denominations and people who do otherwise? Is God's calling to be healing communities only for us Christians? What about the rest of the world, and especially people of other faith communities?

Exodus 35:20-29

The second text proposed for study is from the same book in Hebrew scripture. The people of God are still in the dessert (they spent forty years there!). They had received the whole instruction from God through Moses at Sinai and had already experienced

God's wrath and forgiveness following their disobedience in worshipping the golden calf.

Read Exodus 35: 4-9, 10-19, 20-29, 35:30-36:1, 36:2-7 to have an idea of the subject matter.

Many people regard chapters 35 to 40 in Exodus as extremely boring. They are repetitive of chapters 25-31 and technical, yes. Yet they are there in our Bible! As one Christian commentary puts it, they are about "Israel in an advent mode",[2] in a time of waiting, and that is important.

Question 4: Turn to Exodus 35:20-29, a section without parallel. Here there is an invitation to different people to participate in constructing and adorning God's sanctuary! What are the characteristics of this invitation and its response in terms of groups of people? Who responds, and how?

I chose these verses for several reasons; one is that most commentators and preachers ignore them, thus making them invisible to us; second, it would seem in these verses that there is no gender barrier when it comes to serving God with our talents and skills: v. 22 states clearly that *both men and women* brought objects of gold according to the will of their hearts. At this point, the sanctuary is not barred to women! Furthermore, according to v. 25, those women who had weaving ability (literally, "who were wise of heart in their hands") did spin fabrics with their hands, and brought that which they had spun to be used in God's service.

Question 5: What does this text (Ex. 35:20-29) tell you about a healing community and the use of everyone's skills? Can you apply this text in any way to your own community? Why (or why not)?

Notice how here again, as in our previous text, the community's actions (in this case, Israel still in the desert) are directed by God's words, as stated earlier in the book of Exodus, yet they have the freedom of will to respond to God in whatever way their own generosity allows them.

Mark 14:3-9

Turning to the New Testament, we find in the gospels too that there are several stories in which the apostles or others to whom Jesus speaks are challenged when they intend to cut off certain people from Jesus' blessings. One such story appears in

Mark 14:3-9. There, an unnamed woman pours an expensive ointment of nard on Jesus' feet, to which the disciples respond with anger and criticism, but Jesus does not (see especially vs. 4-5). Elsewhere in Mark, the blind man Bartimaeus shouts at Jesus – and Jesus takes notice of him – despite the efforts of others to make him quiet down. In John's gospel, when the disciples come back from a Samaritan town and find Jesus talking at the well with a Samaritan woman, they wonder at his breach in custom but do not say anything.

Question 6: Choose one of these gospel stories, or another one that you remember from the New Testament, and discuss how it affirms the idea of God's community as a healing and reconciling community known for its inclusiveness.

Question 7: As you come to a close in this Bible study, review your answers to the above questions, and seek concrete actions (prayer services, personal or community repentance, gatherings, service ministries) to start to address those aspects of your own community that may not be sufficiently healing and reconciling.

May God bless your reflections, and your actions!

NOTES

[1] Norbert Lohfink, "'I am Yahweh, your Physician' (Exodus 15:26). God, Society and Human Health in a Postexilic Revision of the Pentateuch (Exod. 15:2b,26)", in *Theology of the Pentateuch: Themes of the Priestly Narrative and Deuteronomy*, Minneapolis, Fortress, 1994, pp. 35-95; pp. 35-36, 95 stresses the fact that one of Jesus' main signs in his earthly ministry was healing the sick in order to announce the coming Kingdom of God.

[2] Terence E. Fretheim, *Exodus: Interpretation*, Louisville: John Knox, 1991, p. 313.

Acts 28:25-31 Keith Warrington

So, as they disagreed among themselves, they departed, after Paul had made one statement, 'The Holy Spirit was right in saying to your fathers through Isaiah the prophet: Go to this people, and say, You shall indeed hear but never understand, and you shall indeed see but never perceive. For this people's heart has grown dull, and their ears are heavy of hearing, and their eyes they have closed; lest they should perceive with their eyes, and hear with their ears, and understand with their heart, and turn for me to heal them. Let it be known to you then that this salvation of God has been sent to the Gentiles; they will listen.' And he lived there two whole years at his own expense, and welcomed all who came to him, preaching the kingdom of God and teaching about the Lord Jesus Christ quite openly and unhindered.

These verses conclude the book of Acts and are recorded at the end of two chapters that narrate a sea voyage undertaken by the Apostle Paul. This voyage was to take him from Jerusalem to Rome and would result in his entering a very hostile environment with a message of freedom for people in bondage. Since Paul had been delegated by God for this mission, it was to be expected that evil forces would seek to undermine his plans. However, the story related in the final two chapters of Acts reports that, despite everything that could have resulted in the mission being terminated, Paul arrived safely at his destination and, for two years, engaged in that which God had called him to do (Acts 28:17-28). The reason for this is made clear: God was in charge of the mission. The challenge to the readers of the book is whether they will hear this truth and respond accordingly by committing their lives to the same sovereign Lord who actively directed the destiny of Paul.

Luke deliberately takes a long time detailing the events of the voyage. Indeed, the voyage appears to be more important than other information which he chooses not to record. Thus, he does not record whether Paul met the emperor, whether churches were established by Paul, what happened to Paul during those two years in Rome that are referred to, whether he returned to Antioch or whether he died in Rome. What Luke does record in great detail is the sea voyage from the eastern Mediterranean to Rome ; this is done for a singular purpose, to demonstrate the sovereignty of God who directs the destinies of God's people, ensuring that God's divine will is achieved through them despite every obstacle in the way.

Thus Luke records the problems encountered on the voyage (27:7-28:6), including the slowness and difficulty in sailing caused by the wind, the indecision and unwise actions of the captain, the fierce storm and darkness, the danger of starvation, the potential of the crew abandoning the ship, the shipwreck, the possibility of their being killed by the soldiers and Paul's snakebite. These were all obstacles to be overcome, but none of them was sufficient to disturb God's plans for Paul. The reason is recorded in Acts 27:24 (also 23:11) where Paul states that God had determined that he would stand before Caesar. Therefore, Paul encourages everyone else not to fear because of the trustworthy nature of his God.

This story is particularly significant in its first-century context. The danger of the Mediterranean Sea to the ancients must not be overlooked. The contemporary cruise liners and ferries that sail with modern and accurate maritime aids are very different to the primitive and dangerous conditions of first-century sailing. Another reason for remembering the original context of Paul's voyage relates to the fact that two of the main books used in the schools of the era were the Odyssey (traditionally viewed as being authored by Homer) and Virgil's Aenead. Each was used as a textbook to be read, memorized and dramatized by pupils. In particular, they identified principles of life and conduct, desirable to teach children how to become model citizens. These stories recounted the lives of heroes battling against the odds to cross the Greek (Mediterranean) Sea, overcoming the strategies of various gods, storms and natural enemies along the way, resulting in their achieving their objective. In the Aenead, the prize is viewed as

Rome, settled in by Aeneas and his Trojan companions. The supremacy of the gods supporting these heroes is proven by their ability to support their protégés against all the obstacles facing them.

Luke wrote the book of Acts for mainly Gentile, as well as Jewish, readers. The former were familiar with such epics and the messages they presented. In his account of Paul's sea voyage, Luke demonstrates that the God who protects Paul is superior to all other gods because Paul's God shields him as he crosses the hazardous Greek sea from Israel to Rome. Christian readers can take heart that the God who protected Paul is covenanted to protect them also. At the same time, those whose trust is not in God are encouraged to transfer their allegiance to the one whose authority is supreme. The last verse of the book of Acts emphasizes this unprecedented authority in that Paul is recorded as preaching the kingdom of God and teaching about the Lord Jesus Christ "boldly and without hindrance". The final word in the original Greek is translated "unhindered". Luke's last word on the life of Paul reminds the readers that the one who reigns in supreme power is supervising Paul's destiny and nothing can obstruct God's purpose.

God overshadowed Paul, guiding him and controlling his destiny even in the most unfriendly of circumstances. The same God controls the lives of every other believer. We may not always feel that we have a hold on God, but he always has a hold on us. Christ has ascended, but he is not absent.

Discussion comments

There are a number of challenges relating to the account of Paul's sea voyage for believers.

* When things go wrong, God is still in charge; things do not necessarily go wrong because we have sinned or stepped away from God's will; it is not necessarily that the devil has caused things to go wrong. Often, things go wrong because we are part of a world that has not been right since sin slid into the Garden of Eden. Whatever the cause of our problems, God is not absent from us. The most evil act in history was the crucifixion of Jesus. There, it appeared that God was not in control but that wicked people, operating their

➤

own selfish agenda, were directing the destiny of Jesus. In reality, as Acts 2:23-24 declares, God was still in control. Answers to many of life's problems and traumas are not easily understood. Nevertheless, in the absence of answers, that which is certain is that God is still in charge.

- Safety and security are not found in the absence of danger but in the presence of God. The earliest days of the church saw a devastating catalogue of natural calamities including famines, earthquakes and plagues as well as verbal and physical attacks on Christians resulting in countless martyrdoms. Christians were not safeguarded from the events of that era. What they had to learn was that these events did not separate them from God. The perception of the majority of the people of the day was that the gods were not interested in the situations of people, let alone bothered to involve themselves in their lives. The message of the Bible is that God is so interested in this world that God the Son came into this world in the person of Jesus to demonstrate God's desire to infuse us with the divine, loving presence and all the resources we require. God's purpose is to make a difference to our lives and to the situations in which we find ourselves.

- God holds our future destiny secure, whatever it might be, be it life or death, a pension or martyrdom. God is in control and never out of control. There's never a panic in heaven. God is in control even when it feels as if no one is in control. God is looking after us even though it feels that no one is looking after us. God is determined to provide for us that which is best for us and to fulfil the divine will in our lives. God's authority determines that, as the Psalmist declares, "The Lord does whatever pleases him, in the heavens and on the earth" (135:6). Paul affirms that God is committed to ensuring the completion of that which has been started in our lives (Phil 1:6) while Peter confirms, "You are kept by the power of God" (1 Pet. 1:5). ➤

- The challenge for believers is not only to impress these truths in our own minds but also to present them to an unbelieving world in ways that will enable others to adopt them, as well as accepting the God who makes all things possible as their own guide in life.

Questions

- In what ways does the following blank verse clarify the role of God in the direction of our lives?

One day it did: tired of holding, it let go
and prepared to flutter down
to the dirt below where it knew it would die.

But the wind that had gently plucked it from the tree
tucked it under its arm and took it high: far higher
than ever it had dreamed it could go.

Once it was tied to the tree
but now it was free on the breeze.

"Lord, I wish I was that leaf: I wish I could trust you that
completely: to know you hold me – and sense your peace.
But, I'm afraid Lord: afraid to let go: I fear the future:
where I might go: what if I fail: what will letting go
entail, Lord?"

"Son: Trust in My Spirit; the Breeze.
His love for you is what sets you free.
He says that He'll change you – but love is His mould.
He promises to hold you – but tight in His fold.
He promises to use you – but it's all in His love.
You'll fly – but remember your teacher's a dove.
And together you'll fly in peace on the breeze.
His love for you is what gives you peace.
For my will for you is neither a sigh nor a rod;
it's a song ... to take you high, to me, your God.
My Spirit in you is all you need
to know I love you for all eternity.
All I ask of you is to surrender your fears to Me."

➤

- When or where do you find it easiest to listen to God?
- How do you listen for God to speak to you?
- Share an example or experience of your receiving God's guidance.
- What guidance would you give to a new believer in how to listen for/to God?
- How would you help an enquiring unbeliever to recognize that God desires to have a positive influence on the direction of his or her life?

3 *Healing in a World of Exclusion and Violence*

Ephesians 1-3 A.C. Oomen

Reconciliation and healing in a world of exclusion and violence

Consider the following outline of Paul's letter to the church at Ephesus:

1. *God's plan for the world* : *Ephesians 1*

Paul, an apostle of Christ Jesus by the will of God, to the saints who are in Ephesus and are faithful in Christ Jesus: Grace to you and peace from God our Father and the Lord Jesus Christ. Blessed be the God and Father of our Lord Jesus Christ, who has blessed us in Christ with every spiritual blessing in the heavenly places, just as he chose us in Christ before the foundation of the world to be holy and blameless before him in love. He destined us for adoption as his children through Jesus Christ, according to the good pleasure of his will, to the praise of his glorious grace that he freely bestowed on us in the Beloved. In him we have redemption through his blood, the forgiveness of our trespasses, according to the riches of his grace that he lavished on us. With all wisdom and insight he has made known to us the mystery of his will, according to his good pleasure that he set forth in Christ, as a plan for the fullness of time, to gather up all things in him, things in heaven and things on earth. In Christ we have also obtained an inheritance, having been destined according to the purpose of him who accomplishes all things according to his counsel and will, so that we, who were the first to set our hope on Christ, might live for the praise of his glory. In him you also, when you had heard the word of truth, the gospel of your salvation, and had believed in him, were marked with the seal of the promised Holy Spirit; this is the pledge of our inheritance toward redemption as God's own people, to the praise of his glory. I have heard of your faith in the Lord Jesus and your love toward all the saints, and for this reason I do not cease to give thanks for you as I remember you in my prayers. I pray that the God of our Lord Jesus Christ, the Father of glory, may give you a spirit of wisdom and revelation as you come to know him, so that, with the eyes of your heart enlightened, you may know what is the hope to which he has called you, what are the riches of his glorious inheritance among the saints, and what is the immeasurable greatness of his power for us who believe, according to the working of his great power. God put this power to work in Christ when he raised him from the dead and seated him at his right hand in the heavenly places, far above all rule and authority and power and dominion, and above every name that is named, not only in this age but also in the age to come. And he has put all things under his feet and has made him the head over all things for the church, which is his body, the fullness of him who fills all in all.

God's design:

Paul has two essential messages of good news – one expressed most carefully in his letter to the Romans: Justification by faith. Second, through Ephesians we discover the Pauline understanding of God's plan for universal salvation: Reuniting all things through Christ. In the first chapter of Ephesians, Paul describes God's design.

1. God had this plan in mind even when laying the foundation of the creation. It was kept a secret, a mystery, even from the angels. In the fullness of time, God has revealed it.

2. God's design is revealed in Jesus Christ, so that in and through him the whole creation will be reconciled and brought to a unity and harmony. The life, work, teaching, death and resurrection of Jesus thus was not an isolated event at a certain date in history but an event of universal significance, forming the centre and focus of God's action in this world.

3. The majesty of God's plan is that it takes into account every created being including the believers in Ephesus and other churches. All believers are reconciled into one body and also are instruments for reconciliation. This explains the identity and mission of the body of Christ.

To ponder

1. Paul starts with the universal and then comes to the particular. The whole pattern is drawn first, as in a jigsaw puzzle, and then the bits are fit into place within the whole. That which is true of all may be demonstrated in the particular.

2. Jesus Christ is the pattern and the centre of the whole fabric. He is both God's mystery and men's and women's salvation. In him, all the universe joins together and, with him as the head, offers eternal sacrifice to the Father.

3. Human beings are defined in terms of this greater significance and purpose. In Jesus Christ, humanity is made whole and restored to the purpose for which God has created man and woman. This is healing or salvation (in Greek, sostham).

Key verses

v. 9: mystery of his plan – a secret now made known

v. 10: gather all things in Christ – IN CHRIST – abiding – dwelling in Christ

v. 13&14: Holy Spirit – the sealing and the first installment (araborn) – safety security.

v. 18: That you may "know" – experience at the depth of your being – reason and revelation.

v. 22&23: The church – Christ's body – filling all things.

Questions for discussion

1. Why is it that we do not often recognize the signs of God gathering all things together in Jesus Christ? Is it that our inner eyes are not yet open?

2. The church is the fullness of him that fills all in all. Where is it? Where do the church's structure and essential being come into conflict?

3. If this is God's design and purpose, how does our exclusiveness affect God's plan? Can we name our exclusion of others as sin – as that which tries to destroy God's plan?

Prayer

Glory and honour to the eternal one sitting on the throne. Thanks and praise to God for Jesus Christ in whom we have inherited our participation in the Spirit's movement towards the unifying of all things.In Christ's name we pray. Amen.

2. *The human predicament* : *Ephesians 2*

*Y*ou *were dead through the trespasses and sins in which you once lived, following the course of this world, following the ruler of the power of the air, the spirit that is now at work among those who are disobedient. All of us once lived among them in the passions of our flesh, following the desires of flesh and senses, and we were by nature children of wrath, like everyone else. But God, who is rich in mercy, out of the great love with which he loved us even when we were dead through our trespasses, made us alive together with Christ – by grace you have been saved – and raised us up with him and seated us with him in the heavenly places in Christ Jesus, so that in the ages to come he might show the immeasurable riches of his grace in kindness toward us in Christ Jesus. For by grace you have been saved through faith, and this is not your own doing; it is the gift of God – not the result of works, so that no one may boast. For we are what he has made us, created in Christ Jesus for good works, which God prepared beforehand to be our way of life. So then, remember that at one time you Gentiles by birth, called "the uncircumcision" by those who are called "the circumcision" – a physical circumcision made in the flesh by human hands – remember that you were at that time without Christ, being aliens from the commonwealth of Israel, and strangers to the covenants of promise, having no hope and without God in the world. But now in Christ Jesus you who once were far off have been brought near by the blood of Christ. For he is our peace; in his flesh he has made both groups into one and has broken down the dividing wall, that is, the hostility between us. He has abolished the law with its commandments and ordinances, that he might create in himself one new humanity in place of the two, thus making peace, and might reconcile both groups to God in one body through the cross, thus putting to death that hostility through it. So he came and proclaimed peace to you who were far off and peace to those who were near; for through him both of us have access in one Spirit to the Father. So then you are no longer strangers and aliens, but you are citizens with the saints and also members of the household of God, built upon the foundation of the apostles and prophets, with Christ Jesus himself as the cornerstone. In him the* *whole structure is joined together and grows into a holy temple in the Lord; in whom you also are built together spiritually into a dwelling place for God.*

Paul speaks in uncompromising words about the condition this world is in. What we were as created humanity, before the fall, is in direct contrast with what we are. No attempt at rationalizing, compromising and explaining away the fall of the human race, in cultural and ethnic terms, will remove the depth to which we have fallen. An acceptance of this leads us to a broken and contrite heart and to receive, at the foot of the cross, a new and totally different way of life. The picture drawn is both individual and collective – of each of us as persons, and of all of us as a community. Look at the words the author uses – "dead in trespasses and sins", "walk according to the course of this world", "the prince of the air", "the lust of our flesh", "children of wrath" – these words are deep and penetrating.

As deep as was our fall, so great is God's love. God bestows redemption on us freely. All this demonstrates God's plan of universal reconciliation. The path through which God achieved the bringing together of all came first by creating one New Humanity and then breaking down all the middle walls of partition that divide person from person. The cross is the foundation of this unity. We approach God the Father, through the Holy Spirit, at the cross of Christ. The process of reconciliation still continues.

Some important verses

1. Reality of the old nature – old world v. 1-3; and the transformation, v. 4-7.

2. v. 8-10: A short summary of the experience of salvation.

3. v. 13&14: In Christ – the heart of Paul's theology: peace, breaking down walls as already having been accomplished in him.

4. v. 19-22: Secret of growth in the body of Christ – "Become what you are!"

To ponder

1. To name SIN as real and serious, cutting through the inner being of persons and communities, is necessary to recognize if we are to enter freely into the experience of being forgiven. Attempts at calling sin by any other, lighter name will mean only that we deceive ourselves.

2. The love of God is far greater than any sense of our unworthiness. Justification, therefore, is by faith not by works. We are children of grace.

3. People and society are created for good works, plans for which have already been laid by God. If we obey God's plans, unity and reconciliation are guaranteed. And we will have the joy of knowing that our lives are significant and sacred as instruments in God's hands.

Questions

1. Can we trace the malice in our world today, and in persons and families, to its real root cause of alienation from God, and recognize malice as sin which can be overcome only by the blood of Christ on the cross at Calvary?

2. The worth of a human being often is calculated today in terms of money, position, influence etc. Can we acknowledge and admit our mistake in judging according to these measures, saying boldly that our worth is based on the Almighty's reconciling us to God and to one another, and assigning us a role in the reconciliation of the world to God?

3. "Household of God" – Is that not what the church is called to be? The foundation is historic: the cornerstone, Jesus Christ. This household is a building fitly framed together – growing into a holy temple in the Lord. Does that describe the church we know? If not, we should check where we have gone wrong.

Prayer

We praise you, Lord, from the depth of our being, for your abundant love, which you have shown to us by cleansing us and building us together into your holy temple, a household of faith. Forgive us our lapses. Heal us, and build us up by your grace, through Jesus Christ our Lord. Amen.

3. *Therefore, the task ahead* : *Ephesians 3*

This is the reason that I Paul am a prisoner for Christ Jesus for the sake of you Gentiles – for surely you have already heard of the commission of God's grace that was given me for you, and how the mystery was made known to me by revelation, as I wrote above in a few words, a reading of which will enable you to perceive my understanding of the mystery of Christ. In former generations this mystery was not made known to humankind, as it has now been revealed to his holy apostles and prophets by the Spirit: that is, the Gentiles have become fellow heirs, members of the same body, and sharers in the promise in Christ Jesus through the gospel. Of this gospel I have become a servant according to the gift of God's grace that was given me by the working of his power. Although I am the very least of all the saints, this grace was given to me to bring to the Gentiles the news of the boundless riches of Christ, and to make everyone see what is the plan of the mystery hidden for ages in God who created all things; so that through the church the wisdom of God in its rich variety might now be made known to the rulers and authorities in the heavenly places. This was in accordance with the eternal purpose that he has carried out in Christ Jesus our Lord, in whom we have access to God in boldness and confidence through faith in him. I pray therefore that you may not lose heart over my sufferings for you; they are your glory. For this reason I bow my knees before the Father, from whom every family in heaven and on earth takes its name. I pray that, according to the riches of his glory, he may grant that you may be strengthened in your inner being with power through his Spirit, and that Christ may dwell in your hearts through faith, as you are being rooted and grounded in love. I pray that you may have the power to comprehend, with all the saints, what is the breadth and length and height and depth, and to know the love of Christ that surpasses knowledge, so that you may be filled with all the fullness of God. Now to him who by the power at work within us is able to accomplish abundantly far more than all we can ask or imagine, to him be glory in the church and in Christ Jesus to all generations, forever and ever. Amen.

Paul brings up his own role as an illustration of how human beings participate in the divine design, despite the context of the human predicament of sin. At a significant point in history, Paul played a role in liberating the church from being seen as a mere sect within the Jewish faith. As an apostle, he set off into the wide world to reveal God's wisdom. In doing so, in all humility, he helped to disclose God's great design for coming generations.

God's plan is to unite all things in Christ and all who accept their role in the church, the body of Christ, discover this intention. He calls us to become fully engaged, bold and courageous in the face of frustrations and persecutions. What else can we do now, except to bow in prayer before God the Father of our Lord Jesus Christ, and ask that the indwelling presence of Jesus be in all, so that we may have a glimpse of his love above everything else?

Verses to note

1. v. 8&9: the unsearchable riches of Christ – a key topic in Paul's preaching.
2. v. 11: the wisdom of God – the plan is to be known to all.
3. Prayer: v. 14-19
    a) To be strengthened in the inner person.
    b) Christ may dwell in your hearts by faith – which is healing.
    c) Prayer, v. 14-19 – to know God's love.
    d) Filled with all the fullness of God.

To ponder

1. God acts in history to bring history to a focus point, so that history has meaning, purpose and direction. History is a dialogue between God and humanity. That is the way in which history should be interpreted.
2. To understand this unique plan of God, one has to take his/her stand along with fellow believers within the unity of Christ's body the Church. The role of the church is to reveal God's plan to the world through believers. This is mission.
3. In taking this stand with the multitude who are called, we experience the indwelling presence of Christ through the Holy Spirit. This is healing, health and wholeness. Physical well-being contributes to this, but it is not identical to wholeness – which is salvation, discovering the true meaning and purpose of life.

Questions

1. If healing is wholeness, it is necessary that the ministry of the church should proclaim removal of all divine walls of partition caused by caste, creed, colour or culture. Can we then assert that any such divisions we may see within the church are a denial of the very nature of Christ's body, and so are sinful?
2. Where do we start building up unity – in persons, family, church, world?
3. What practical steps may we take to re-assert the wholistic, unifying nature of our mission – on the personal and community levels?

Prayer

Abide in us, O Lord, that we may increasingly abide in you. And thus, while experiencing wholeness in community with others, may we proclaim and demonstrate to the world the unity and reconciliation you have offered freely to us and to the rest of mankind. Turn us from patterns of strife and exclusion, and make us one in Jesus Christ, in whose name we pray. Amen.

John 8:1-11,
Acts 7:54-59,
1 Peter 2:4-10   Aino Nenola and Riina Nguyen

*T*hen *each of them went home, while Jesus went to the Mount of Olives. Early in the morning he came again to the temple. All the people came to him and he sat down and began to teach them. The scribes and the Pharisees brought a woman who had been caught in adultery; and making her stand before all of them, they said to him, "Teacher, this woman was caught in the very act of committing adultery. Now in the law Moses commanded us to stone such women. Now what do you say?" They said this to test him, so that they might have some charge to bring against him. Jesus bent down and wrote with his finger on the ground. When they kept on questioning him, he straightened up and said to them, "Let anyone among you who is without sin be the first to throw a stone at her." And once again he bent down and wrote on the ground. When they heard it, they went away, one by one, beginning with the elders; and Jesus was left alone with the woman standing before him. Jesus straightened up and said to her, "Woman, where are they? Has no one condemned you?" She said, "No one, sir." And Jesus said, "Neither do I condemn you. Go your way, and from now on do not sin again." (John 8:1-11)*

When they heard these things, they became enraged and ground their teeth at Stephen. But filled with the Holy Spirit, he gazed into heaven and saw the glory of God and Jesus standing at the right hand of God. "Look," he said, "I see the heavens opened and the Son of Man standing at the right hand of God!" But they covered their ears, and with a loud shout all rushed together against him. Then they dragged him out of the city and began to stone him; and the witnesses laid their coats at the feet of a young man named Saul. While they were stoning Stephen, he prayed, "Lord Jesus, receive my spirit." Acts 7:54-59)

Come to him, a living stone, though rejected by mortals yet chosen and precious in God's sight, and like living stones, let yourselves be built into a spiritual house, to be a holy priesthood, to offer spiritual sacrifices acceptable to God through Jesus Christ. For it stands in scripture: "See, I am laying in Zion a stone, a cornerstone chosen and precious; and whoever believes in him will not be put to shame." "To you then who believe, he is precious; but for those who do not believe, the stone that the builders rejected has become the very head of the corner," and "A stone that makes them stumble, and a rock that makes them fall." They stumble because they disobey the word, as they were destined to do. But you are a chosen race, a royal priesthood, a holy nation, God's own people, in order that you may proclaim the mighty acts of him who called you out of darkness into his marvelous light. Once you were not a people, but now you are God's people; once you had not received mercy, but now you have received mercy. (1 Peter 2:4-10)

The symbolism of stone

A stone may be seen just as a small and insignificant object. We step on pebbles and stones every day. On the other hand, stone, or rock, is definitely a solid natural reserve. It can protect us from the elements and form a strong foundation or building material in construction. Or one can use stone as an image of hard times and ordeals, as the saying "a stony path" illustrates. One finds these meanings, and more, in the Holy Bible.

David carried stones as weapons in his bag to confront Goliath. Jacob used a stone as a pillow, before it became a sign of God's promise given in his dream and the pillar of God's house. In another passage, one builder built his house on sand and it was destroyed by a storm. But the other built on a rock, and his house was saved. Evil gave Jesus a hard time, tempting him in the wilderness where he was surrounded by sand and pebbles. "Command that these stones become bread," Evil insisted, but Jesus replied: "Man shall not live by bread alone, but by every word that proceeds from the mouth of God" (Matt. 4:3-4).

Stoning – a horrifying practice found even in the Bible – has a variety of characteristics. From difficult biblical narratives there arise profound ethical questions, as well as a different symbolism based on stone. Beyond this, the apostolic metaphor of Christ as "the cornerstone" draws us onward to spiritual growth and renewal.

Stoning narratives

John 8:1-11

Two stoning narratives are represented in these New Testament texts. First, in the gospel account, Christ is asked to pass judgment on a woman who is accused of adultery. The scribes and Pharisees refer to the Law of Moses, which they interpret as condemning her to suffer the penalty of stoning. The Ten Commandments – written on stone – clearly forbid adultery. What does Jesus, who did not come to abolish but to fulfil the Law (Matt. 5:17), reply to them? He states: "He who is without sin among you, let him throw a stone at her first."

And what happens? One by one, they leave, since no one can claim to be without sin. Christ, who never sinned but was endlessly merciful, does not condemn her either. Nevertheless, Jesus does not send the woman away without direction or guidance. He tells her not to sin again. This is not to be taken lightly, but very seriously. The love and mercy of God are never-ending, but at the same time we possess freedom to assume responsibility for our own actions. The woman is called to be a responsible person, to sin no more in order to become a truly free human being. Violence and force are not the means to achieve goodness: love and mercy are the proper means.

Acts 7:54-59

Second, in Acts 7, we find that powerful sermons by Stephen, one of the first deacons of the church, have infuriated the members of the governing council. But Stephen does not cease proclaiming and praying. Consequently, he is dragged out of the city to be stoned. One witness to this was Saul, who at the time accepted these violent actions - but later he came to be known as the apostle Paul, a passionate defender of Christ and his teaching.

While being stoned, Stephen continues praying. He prays not only for himself but for those taking his life. "Lord, do not charge them with this sin." With these words, he shows love and mercy for his enemies, exactly as Jesus taught and said himself on the cross.

In these stories, stone becomes the occasion for a revelation of God's power. In the first story, the presence of stone reveals to people their own sinful state; in the second narrative, stone aids in revealing to witnesses the sanctity of Stephen. On the other hand, in these passages stone is an instrument of execution, even though it may become a sign of repentance when dropped from one's hand to the ground. Stoning gives individual executioners the possibility of remaining anonymous murderers. Human stupidity, cruelty and cowardice are crystallized in stoning – one can claim: "It was not I who killed her: I threw only one stone." Christ asks who will throw the first stone. He asks us this question every day, because stoning is still part of our life. A stone can take different forms – it can be a cruel word, a slap on face, an aggressive attitude, a kick or hit, harassment; the list in endless.

We condemn others so easily without any comprehension of our sinful behaviour, just casually talking and thinking. We may be like those stoning Stephen, or like those accusing the woman and then realizing their own sinful state, or like the woman who sinned but was forgiven, or like Stephen who prayed for his executors. We can choose a heart of flesh instead of a stony heart. As Ecclesiastes says, there is "a time to cast away stones, and a time to gather stones together" (Eccl. 3:5). We can choose not to throw the first stone, nor the last. Making decisions and choices for better is not only ethical, but also a profound sign of our common humanity that reaches towards the original beauty of God's creation.

Christ the cornerstone

1 Peter 2:4-10
We often think that stone is dead, unchanging material. It is timeless, strong and long lasting. In the Bible we can find another dimension · stone is also living, alive. The apostle Peter calls us to come to God "as to a living stone, rejected indeed by men, but chosen by God and precious, you also, as living stones, are being built up a spiritual house, a holy priesthood, to offer up spiritual sacrifices acceptable to God through Jesus Christ". This passage seems to be the culmination of biblical stone narratives. What we might have thought to be dead is more alive than anything. God in Jesus Christ is the living cornerstone – not only of the church but of the whole universe, of everything that is created. Christ is a living stone and we are called to become the same.

But how can this happen? We remember the prophecy of Ezekiel in which God says Israel will become God's own people when "I will remove the heart of stone from their bodies and I will give them a heart of flesh." (Ezek. 11:19) And it is only then that we will become God's people. In a mysterious way God becomes a living stone – and even more mysteriously it seems that our shriveled hearts may again become alive.

We all have our heavy stones to carry. A week before his passion, death and resurrection Christ confronted a heavy stone. It was the stone at the entrance to the tomb of his friend Lazarus. Christ asked the stone to be rolled away and called Lazarus back to life. By this incomprehensible miracle, Christ foretold his own resurrection.

As we build, with ourselves as living stones, and gather around Christ the cornerstone, we nevertheless are striving with our stony hearts. At the very moment we realize our burden we can see that the stone has already been rolled away. To illustrate this, let us remember yet another passage from the gospels. There were women who loved the Lord and also had a stone to struggle with. It was a very large stone... On the sunrise of first day of the week, very early in the morning, myrrh-bearing women went to the tomb of Christ. "They had been asking each other, "Who will roll away the stone for us from the entrance to the tomb?" But when they looked up, they saw that the stone, which was very large, had been rolled back" (Mark 16:1-4). This stone revealed the secret of life: resurrection of the promise that has been present from creation.

Topics for discussion

In the group, think about your home and the meaning of stone in your community. What is the first thought that comes to your mind? Perhaps your church is built of stone, or you have a stone cross there?

Choose one of the stoning or cornerstone narratives in this study, and go it by reading with the group (aloud or silently).

1. Stoning: Acts 7:54-59: Stephen; John 8:1-11: the accused adulteress

– What is the story line of each story, and are they somehow comparable?
– What does stone serve to reveal in these narratives, and how? ➤

- What has stoning to do with our time: why are these narratives still meaningful to us?
- What is there in Christ's approach to a sinner that is ultimately different or new?

2. *Cornerstone – 1 Peter 2:4-8: Living stones*
- What is a cornerstone in real life? Discuss the use of stones in a building.
- Why, then, are we called living stones, and Christ the cornerstone?
- What is the nature of the house of which we are stones and Christ is the cornerstone?
- How do you understand our spiritual growth in becoming living stones?

Pictures for contemplation:
- icon of St. Stephen
- stones

John 8:1-11   Daisy L. Machado

Then each of them went home, while Jesus went to the Mount of Olives. Early in the morning he came again to the temple. All the people came to him and he sat down and began to teach them. The scribes and the Pharisees brought a woman who had been caught in adultery; and making her stand before all of them, they said to him, "Teacher, this woman was caught in the very act of committing adultery. Now in the law Moses commanded us to stone such women. Now what do you say?" They said this to test him, so that they might have some charge to bring against him. Jesus bent down and wrote with his finger on the ground. When they kept on questioning him, he straightened up and said to them, "Let anyone among you who is without sin be the first to throw a stone at her." And once again he bent down and wrote on the ground. When they heard it, they went away, one by one, beginning with the elders; and Jesus was left alone with the woman standing before him. Jesus straightened up and said to her, "Woman, where are they? Has no one condemned you?" She said, "No one, sir." And Jesus said, "- Neither do I condemn you. Go your way, and from now on do not sin again."

This narrative, commonly known as "The Woman Taken in Adultery", has what biblical scholar Gail O'Day calls a "complicated textual history". This is because the passage was not found in the earliest Greek manuscripts of John and is considered by scholars to have been inserted by scribes or editors in a later period. However, scholars do agree that this story is part of what is known as the "Jesus tradition", and it held great meaning for the early Christian community. It is a delicate and provocative story that unfolds in three scenes and clearly shows the mercy and hope that Jesus offers.

In the first scene, the Pharisees bring the woman who has been caught in adultery to Jesus and ask that he sit as judge in her case (8:3-5). In the second scene, Jesus bends down to write on the ground with his finger (v. 6). He refuses to fall into the trap set for him, and when he stands up to address the Pharisees directly (v. 7) he challenges them to show their sinless nature by throwing the first stone at the woman. The third scene begins in v. 8 when Jesus again bends to write in the dirt on the ground as the crowd departs, leaving him alone with the woman. In his conversation with the woman, Jesus tells her she is free to go when he says, "Neither do I condemn you. Go your way, and from now on sin no more" (v. 11).

A careful reading of the text makes it clear that Jesus is not only concerned with the woman, he is also concerned with the Pharisees who brought her to him to be judged and condemned. His words to the Pharisees, "Let anyone among you who is without sin be the first to throw the stone at her" (v. 7) challenges the way the crowd is actually living their lives, and in saying this Jesus is calling them to accountability. And his words to the woman, "...from now on sin no more" (v. 11), are an invitation to all parties to enter into a new way of life. In Jesus' words and teaching, both the present and the future are addressed. The present with its failings, betrayals, temptations, selfishness and blind self-righteousness are examined, challenged and found wanting. Jesus knew that everyone standing before him had in some way failed. However, he offers all of us the hope of renewal. There is no need to repeat the past filled with anger and condemnation, and no need to live in the present with guilt and shame. In the new kingdom there is always the opportunity to sin no more, to live a life of renewal and change, of hope and restoration.

Reflection

Despite the great hope and mercy found in this story, there remains the undeniable tension that the text can be read from a narrow perspective in which the focus may be kept on the woman and her sin. The fact that the woman who is brought before Jesus was being humiliated and was identified by the Pharisees as the object and source of the problem must be considered. She was the one accused of adultery, even though the act of adultery requires two persons. She was the one brought before Jesus naked, caught in the act, while one is left to wonder where her lover was at that moment and what he was wearing. Was he given the opportunity to quickly dress and run away, while the woman was not? The fact that the religious rage of the Pharisees focused on the woman reminds us how through the centuries and even today women remain vulnerable to the violence of the patriarchal, or male-dominated, systems—cultural, political, economic, religious—that continue to function around the globe. As I read this story I am especially reminded of the violence faced by the immigrant women who live and die along the United States-Mexico border. Because I live in the state of Texas, which shares a border with Mexico, I am only too aware of how much violence, especially against women, takes place in that region. And what I am especially aware of is how much that violence is tied to the issue of globalization and the free-market economy that flourishes without constraints on both sides of the U.S.-Mexico border. Globalization, too, is full of unequal relationships, including relations between men and women, as well as questionable assumptions on the part of leaders.

Let me invite you to think about globalization on two levels. For example, we must acknowledge the fact that multinational corporations do have the potential to influence both political and economic life in all corners of the globe. According to Forbes magazine, the largest multinational corporations, such as General Motors, Ford and Mitsubishi, enjoy total sales that exceed the gross domestic product of all but the most productive nations in the world.[1] This is the numerical side of globalization that is so very important and merits careful analysis. However, as Christians I want us to examine another equally important side of globalization.

In order to move towards a faith-inspired vision of globalization, we must ask two very basic but crucial questions: Who are the victims of globalization? And, why are women especially vulnerable to the forces of globalization? I am asking these questions so that we may examine two important Christian concerns: the unity of the human family, and the situation of the poor in the context of our lived reality. Our concerns for unity and the poor develop from our understanding that we have been called and enabled by God to be defenders of what is just, and to be instruments to promote that justice right where we live. It is clear that "the benefits of globalization do not extend to all countries or social groups. Indeed, the dramatic extremes of wealth and poverty born of globalization menace both democracy and social stability in various regions [of the world]."² This is shown by the fact that "by some estimates roughly a fifth of the world's population lives in absolute poverty, bringing fear, early death, squalid living conditions and disease."³

One of the most powerful economic forces along the U.S.-Mexico border is the *maquiladora* industry. The Mexican government established the in-bound *maquiladora* or twin plant programme in 1965 as the Border Industrialization Plan. This programme allowed foreign companies to establish highly competitive manufacturing and production facilities in Mexico and ship raw materials and components to those facilities under special tariffs and oftentimes tariff-free.⁴ The many workers I have met through the years share a similar story: they work a 40-50 hour week for a salary that can run anywhere from $25-50 U.S. dollars. More than 80 percent of *maquiladora* workers are women from the ages of 16 to 24, and sexual harassment as well as loss of employment because of pregnancy are common experiences. The movement of so many young women from rural communities in the interior of Mexico to the border region to work in the *maquiladoras* has also made them vulnerable to sexual predators and physical abuse. The most blatant example of this disregard for the safety and welfare of these immigrant women is made obvious by the "femicide" that has been a reality in Ciudad Juárez, a border city in Mexico. From 1993 to the end of 2001, 259 women between the ages of 17 to 25 have been murdered. Another sad piece in this unsolved femicide, for which the Mexican government has failed to bring anyone to justice, is that most if not all of the women were *maquiladora* workers. The globalization of the Mexican border with its inherent idea of the "disposable" worker makes the unresolved deaths of these women even more tragic and morally reprehensible. The issue here is that the governments of both the United States and Mexico fail to accept any moral responsibility for the loss of life of these immigrant women who are either trying to find employment or are trying to find a way to come across to *el norte*. Another important problem related to immigration in the U.S. borderlands is that of human trafficking, especially of young girls and women, for the sex trade. The news report in 2003 has revealed the bringing in of about thirty-nine women from Honduras who were supposedly contracted to come and work in restaurants in Fort Worth and Dallas, Texas – but were really being brought in for prostitution. These sad stories have been repeated in other states like Florida, and as far north as Massachusetts. The reality that immigrants continue to die of thirst in the desert (again, the majority are women and children) or suffocate in storage containers becomes a paramount concern for those who struggle with the moral realities related to immigration from Mexico into the United States. The issues of violence against immigrants as well as the vulnerability of the female immigrant need to be continually uplifted and proclaimed. This also means is that a core issue that must be critically examined if one is to engage in a theological and ethical analysis of immigration into the U.S. (or any other first-world nation) is that of the protection of white or Euro-American privilege.

There is also the gendered dimension to globalization as well as to the issues of immigration and violence against many women migrants. The necessity to provide for food, housing, clothing and other basic needs continues to fuel the migration of women around the globe, yet the perils they face remain invisible to most of us who live in the comfort of over-developed and wealthy societies. When these immigrant women are brought before us, they are presented to us as illegal immigrants who are guilty of disrespecting immigration laws, who come to take what is not theirs by citizenship. They are presented to us as interlopers and usurpers who are illiterate and unskilled and who will become a burden to our system of social services. They are presented to us as less deserving because they are outside the law. Yet as Jesus stands with us looking upon the many immigrant women (and men) who cross borders around the world, he does not condemn them, he does not reject them, he does not turn them away. And in his acceptance of them he has given them and us hope. Jesus has welcomed all, and in that welcome has proclaimed our common worth and dignity. But even more than that, in his welcome and acceptance he has also given us the opportunity for repentance and renewal. The question remains: will we continue to turn away, or will seek change and renewal?

Activities

View a documentary

The issue of immigration and illegal immigrants is often filled with emotions, negative and positive, on both sides of the debate. However, what is often ignored in the debate is the vulnerability and peril immigrants, especially women, often face. Invite a group of folks from your congregation to view the documentary *Señorita Extraviada* that examines the deaths of the young women of Ciudad Juárez, Mexico. Prepare questions for group discussion after the film is viewed, and provide fact sheets about the reality of the *maquiladora* industry in Mexico. The video can be obtained from: Women Make Movies, www.wmm.com, or in North America you can call (212) 925-0606.

NOTES

[1] Douglas A. Hicks, "Thinking Globally," in *The Christian Century*, December 12, 2001, p. 14.

[2] Yersu Kim, "Philosophy and the Prospects for a Universal Ethics," in *Religion and Globalization*, vol. 1, Max Stackhouse and Peter Paris eds, Harrisburg, Trinity Press, 2000, p. 77.

[3] William Schweiker, "Responsibility in the World of Mammmon"in *Religion and Globalisation*, p. 105.

[4] www.tnrcc.state.tx.us/exec/oppr/border/border.html

4 *Christian Communities in Globalized World*

James 1-5   Daisy L. Machado

*J*ames, a servant of God and of the Lord Jesus Christ, to the twelve
tribes in the Dispersion: Greetings. My brothers and sisters, whenever you face trials of any kind, consider it nothing but joy, because
you know that the testing of your faith produces endurance; and let
endurance have its full effect, so that you may be mature and complete, lacking in nothing. If any of you is lacking in wisdom, ask
God, who gives to all generously and ungrudgingly, and it will be
given you. But ask in faith, never doubting, for the one who doubts
is like a wave of the sea, driven and tossed by the wind; for the
doubter, being double-minded and unstable in every way, must not
expect to receive anything from the Lord. Let the believer who is
lowly boast in being raised up, and the rich in being brought low,
because the rich will disappear like a flower in the field. For the sun
rises with its scorching heat and withers the field; its flower falls,
and its beauty perishes. It is the same way with the rich; in the
midst of a busy life, they will wither away. Blessed is anyone who
endures temptation. Such a one has stood the test and will receive
the crown of life that the Lord has promised to those who love him.
No one, when tempted, should say, "I am being tempted by God";
for God cannot be tempted by evil and he himself tempts no one. But
one is tempted by one's own desire, being lured and enticed by it;
then, when that desire has conceived, it gives birth to sin, and that
sin, when it is fully grown, gives birth to death. Do not be deceived,
my beloved. Every generous act of giving, with every perfect gift, is
from above, coming down from the Father of lights, with whom
there is no variation or shadow due to change. In fulfillment of his
own purpose he gave us birth by the word of truth, so that we would
become a kind of first fruits of his creatures. You must understand
this, my beloved: let everyone be quick to listen, slow to speak, slow
to anger; for your anger does not produce God's righteousness.

Therefore rid yourselves of all sordidness and rank growth of wickedness, and welcome with meekness the implanted word that has the power to save your souls. But be doers of the word, and not merely hearers who deceive themselves. For if any are hearers of the word and not doers, they are like those who look at themselves in a mirror; for they look at themselves and, on going away, immediately forget what they were like. But those who look into the perfect law, the law of liberty, and persevere, being not hearers who forget but doers who act—they will be blessed in their doing. If any think they are religious, and do not bridle their tongues but deceive their hearts, their religion is worthless. Religion that is pure and undefiled before God, the Father, is this: to care for orphans and widows in their distress, and to keep oneself unstained by the world.

My brothers and sisters, do you with your acts of favoritism really believe in our glorious Lord Jesus Christ? For if a person with gold rings and in fine clothes comes into your assembly, and if a poor person in dirty clothes also comes in, and if you take notice of the one wearing the fine clothes and say, "Have a seat here, please," while to the one who is poor you say, "Stand there," or, "Sit at my feet," have you not made distinctions among yourselves, and become judges with evil thoughts? Listen, my beloved brothers and sisters. Has not God chosen the poor in the world to be rich in faith and to be heirs of the kingdom that he has promised to those who love him ? But you have dishonored the poor. Is it not the rich who oppress you? Is it not they who drag you into court? Is it not they who blaspheme the excellent name that was invoked over you? You do well if you really fulfill the royal law according to the scripture, "You shall love your neighbor as yourself." But if you show partiality, you commit sin and are convicted by the law as transgressors. For whoever keeps the whole law but fails in one point has become accountable for all of it. For the one who said, "You shall not commit adultery," also said, "You shall not murder." Now if you do not commit adultery but if you murder, you have become a transgressor of the law. So speak and so act as those who are to be judged by the law of liberty. For judgment will be without mercy to anyone who has shown no mercy; mercy triumphs over judgment. What good is it, my brothers and sisters, if you say you have faith but do not have works? Can faith save you? If a brother or sister is naked and lacks daily food, and one of you says to them, "Go in peace; keep warm and eat your fill," and yet you do not supply their bodily needs, what is the good of that? So faith by itself, if it has no works, is dead. But someone will say, "You have faith and I have works." Show me your faith apart from your works, and I by my works will show you my faith. You believe that God is one; you do well. Even the demons believe – and shudder. Do you want to be shown, you senseless person, that faith apart from works is barren? Was not our ancestor Abraham justified by works when he offered his son Isaac on the altar? You see that faith was active along with his works, and faith was brought to completion by the works. Thus the scripture was fulfilled that says, "Abraham believed God, and it was reckoned to him as righteousness," and he was called the friend of God. You see that a person is justified by works and not by faith alone. Likewise, was not Rahab the prostitute also justified by works when she welcomed the messengers and sent them out by another road? For just as the body without the spirit is dead, so faith without works is also dead.

Not many of you should become teachers, my brothers and sisters, for you know that we who teach will be judged with greater strictness. For all of us make many mistakes. Anyone who makes no mistakes in speaking is perfect, able to keep the whole body in check with a bridle. If we put bits into the mouths of horses to make them obey us, we guide their whole bodies. Or look at ships: though they are so large that it takes strong winds to drive them, yet they are guided by a very small rudder wherever the will of the pilot directs. So also the tongue is a small member, yet it boasts of great exploits. How great a forest is set ablaze by a small fire! And the tongue is a fire. The tongue is placed among our members as a world of iniquity; it stains the whole body, sets on fire the cycle of nature, and is itself set on fire by hell. For every species of beast and bird, of reptile and sea creature, can be tamed and has been tamed by the human species, but no one can tame the tongue – a restless evil, full of deadly poison. With it we bless the Lord and Father, and with it we curse those who are made in the likeness of God. From the same mouth come blessing and cursing. My brothers and sisters, this ought not to be so. Does a spring pour forth from the same opening both fresh and brackish water? Can a fig tree, my brothers and sisters, yield olives, or a grapevine figs? No more can salt water yield fresh. Who is wise and understanding among you? Show by your good life that your works are done with gentleness born of wisdom. But if you have bitter envy and selfish ambition in your hearts, do not be boastful and false to the truth. Such wisdom does not come down from above, but is earthly, unspiritual, devilish. For where there is envy and selfish ambition, there will also be disorder and wickedness of every kind. But the wisdom from above is first pure, then peaceable, gentle, willing to yield, full of mercy and good fruits, without a trace of partiality or hypocrisy. And a harvest of righteousness is sown in peace for those who make peace.

Those conflicts and disputes among you, where do they come from? Do they not come from your cravings that are at war within you? You want something and do not have it; so you commit murder. And you covet something and cannot obtain it; so you engage in disputes and conflicts. You do not have, because you do not ask. You ask and do not receive, because you ask wrongly, in order to spend what you get on your pleasures. Adulterers! Do you not know that friendship with the world is enmity with God? Therefore whoever wishes to be a friend of the world becomes an enemy of God. Or do you suppose that it is for nothing that the scripture says, "God yearns jealously for the spirit that he has made to dwell in us"? But he gives all the more grace; therefore it says, "God opposes the proud, but gives grace to the humble." Submit yourselves therefore to God. Resist the devil, and he will flee from you. Draw near to God, and he will draw near to you. Cleanse your hands, you sinners, and purify your hearts, you double-minded. Lament and mourn and weep. Let your laughter be turned into mourning and your joy into dejection. Humble yourselves before the Lord, and he will exalt you. Do not speak evil against one another, brothers and sisters. Whoever speaks evil against another or judges another, speaks evil against the law and judges the law; but if you judge the law, you are not a doer of the law but a judge. There is one lawgiver and judge who is able to save and to destroy. So who, then, are you to judge your neighbor? Come now, you who say, "Today or tomorrow we will go to such and such a town and spend a year there, doing business and making money." Yet you do not even know what tomorrow will bring. What is your life? For you are a mist that appears for a little while and then vanishes. Instead you ought to say, "If the Lord wishes, we will live and do this or that." As it is, you boast in your arrogance; all such boasting is evil. Anyone, then, who knows the right thing to do and fails to do it, commits sin.

Come now, you rich people, weep and wail for the miseries that are coming to you. Your riches have rotted, and your clothes are moth-eaten. Your gold and silver have rusted, and their rust will be evidence against you, and it will eat your flesh like fire. You have laid up treasure for the last days. Listen! The wages of the laborers who mowed your fields, which you kept back by fraud, cry out, and the cries of the harvesters have reached the ears of the Lord of hosts. You have lived on the earth in luxury and in pleasure; you have fattened your hearts in a day of slaughter. You have condemned and murdered the righteous one, who does not resist you. Be patient, therefore, beloved, until the coming of the Lord. The farmer waits for the precious crop from the earth, being patient with it until it receives the early and the late rains. You also must be patient. Strengthen your hearts, for the coming of the Lord is near. Beloved, do not grumble against one another, so that you may not be judged. See, the Judge is standing at the doors! As an example of suffering and patience, beloved, take the prophets who spoke in the name of the

Lord. Indeed we call blessed those who showed endurance. You have heard of the endurance of Job, and you have seen the purpose of the Lord, how the Lord is compassionate and merciful. Above all, my beloved, do not swear, either by heaven or by earth or by any other oath, but let your "Yes" be yes and your "No" be no, so that you may not fall under condemnation. Are any among you suffering? They should pray. Are any cheerful? They should sing songs of praise. Are any among you sick? They should call for the elders of the church and have them pray over them, anointing them with oil in the name of the Lord. The prayer of faith will save the sick, and the Lord will raise them up; and anyone who has committed sins will be forgiven. Therefore confess your sins to one another, and pray for one another, so that you may be healed. The prayer of the righteous is powerful and effective. Elijah was a human being like us, and he prayed fervently that it might not rain, and for three years and six months it did not rain on the earth. Then he prayed again, and the heaven gave rain and the earth yielded its harvest. My brothers and sisters, if anyone among you wanders from the truth and is brought back by another, you should know that whoever brings back a sinner from wandering will save the sinner's soul from death and will cover a multitude of sins.

Of the letters by the apostles found in the New Testament, the letter of James is unique in style and composition. This is because of the vague identifications of its author (who is this "James, a servant of God and of the Lord Jesus Christ"?), its audience (who are the "twelve tribes in the Dispersion"?), the occasion for the letter (what led to its writing?) and the fact that it lacks the formal characteristics of a letter. Unlike the other apostolic epistles of the New Testament, in this writing Jesus is mentioned only twice (1:1; 2:1), we find no greetings from the author or anyone else, and the letter does not end with a customary farewell message but ends abruptly and without warning. The body of this writing seems to be composed of a series of wisdom sayings that are often complete unto themselves and were common in pre-Christian Jewish wisdom materials. This is true of chapter 1, which gathers a series of short sayings and teachings that focus on a variety of themes that follow no particular order: trials as a cause of joy (v. 2-4), prayer as the resource for the person who desires wisdom (v. 5-8), the insecurity of a foundation based in riches (v. 9-11), the rewards of the righteous (v. 12), the distinction between temptations and trials (v. 13-15), all that is good comes from God (v. 16-18), the importance of self-control

(v. 19-21), hearing and doing (v. 22-25), the control of the tongue (v. 26), the definition of true religion (v. 27). This same style of using wisdom sayings and teachings is repeated in the concluding section of the epistle, chapter 5:12; 13; 19-20. On the other hand, there are sections of the epistle that are more cohesive and focus on specific concerns in greater detail: the sin of deference towards the rich (2:1-13). faith and works (2:14-26), sins of the tongue (3:1-12), true wisdom (3:13-18), wrongful desires (4:1-10), judgment of the rich (5:1-6), patience of the righteous (5:7-11), the ministry of healing (5:14-18).

The context of the letter

Despite the opinions of some critical commentators through the centuries, the epistle of James is fundamentally a Christian writing addressed to a structured Christian community and written about 80-100 CE. In this epistle the author addresses in a clear and straightforward manner the concrete and familiar ethical problems of the Christian community. He exhorts his fellow Christians not to neglect their obligations to aid those in the community stricken by poverty, he focuses on the relationships to be developed within a community that is to embody the love it professes, and he appeals to those in power within the community, the elders, to minister to the sick through prayer so as to bring healing and forgiveness of sin, and to engage in pastoral efforts to recall the sinner to community. James clearly speaks of the tensions between rich and poor and boldly denounces those merchants who gain their wealth by withholding the wages from workers (5:1-6). He also warns those who have placed their hopes for the future in their possessions and wealth (4:13-17). The author's concern is to promote the development of a community that practices what it preaches, that embodies the ideal it confesses, that truly understands that faith without works is indeed no faith at all so. Like the apostle Paul (Galatians 5:14), James holds that it is in loving one's neighbour that the law is fulfilled (2:8).

Reflection

While many centuries separate the community James wrote to from today's Christian community, the ethical concerns and problems we as Christians face today in our globalized world bear many similarities to the issues and concerns James addressed in his epistle.

When we read James' letter we are reminded that the Christian community is called to live out its faith through relationships that are neither shaped nor governed by the values of the world we live in. Instead we must acknowledge how God through Jesus the Christ "de-centres the centre", making less "central" the places of worldly power, prestige and wealth so that the focus may be on those who have been left out, excluded, devalued, pushed aside, ignored, dismissed, erased from denominational histories and mission statements, assigned to the category of "special ministries" or "special projects", and who have become the focus of the do-gooder charity efforts commonly found in too many churches. The core concepts found in the teachings of James are all about justice and mercy, which must also involve hospitality and healing, and these are what should be at the centre of today's Christian community. The type of community James is inviting us to create is really an invitation into a life of fulfillment in an otherwise vacuous society. I find it interesting that James' core teaching that "faith without words is dead" (2:26) is what Dietrich Bonhoeffer described as the "confessional stance of the church in the world"[1] which for Bonhoeffer was something very specific. Bonhoeffer wrote: "The primary confession of the Christian before the world is the deed which interprets itself...The deed alone is our confession of faith before the world."[2] This is what James wanted his readers to understand.

And so the Christian community of the twenty-first century is called to the deed, to action, that is to "praxis" or practice, which is ultimately the oxygen of our faith. To say yes to this call is to affirm life, it is to be healed and empowered, it is the stirring of the Holy Spirit in our being, it is to be released from fear so that we will not pass judgment. We will not be afraid to risk our lives ; we will be willing to make ourselves vulnerable. Being called to praxis, or Christian action, means that we must be willing to share not because we give from what is left over but because we give of our best, of what is most precious to us. When we respond to the call to an emboldened praxis, to the deed that interprets our faith, we will be able to enter into new depths of sharing, mutual love and exuberant faith. We will be made hungry for the experience of living in Christian love. To respond to this call is to learn to live in true solidarity.

And what is solidarity? Latin American theologian Jon Sobrino defines solidarity as closeness, support and defense of the weak. He says, "Solidarity is the tenderness of peoples."[3]

expressed in tenderness is not a very valuable sentiment in a free-market, globalized economy; however, it must be at the core of Christian behaviour and the Christian community. Solidarity allows us to see the imago dei in the faces of those not like us, and it gives us the strength to reach out to those we consider foreign, to "the other" , and to attempt to build community. And it is solidarity that condemns the radical individualism that pervades the lifestyle we find today throughout those nations that enjoy wealth and power, where the value of a person is measured in how much she or he can buy.

Solidarity demands that today's Christian community continue to state clearly and to uphold the truth that Christianity has a central conviction – that "all reality exists in relation to God as creator, redeemer and sustainer and, in light of this fact, bears inviolable worth... [and even more] that human worth, grounded in a relation to God, cannot be commodified or measured within the discourse of any social sphere."[4] Therefore the task facing the church is that it must transmit this picture of the worth of human life, and enable it to penetrate the global imagination.[5] We are called to see ourselves in the faces of those who live on the margins and on the bottom, and to offer them hospitality and healing. We are called to celebrate the claim that all human beings are God's beloved children. We are called to transmit the meaning of the words of a South African proverb: "A person becomes a person through other persons."

Activities

Praying the world

Take any local or national newspaper and pick out a few headlines or lead articles. These news items then become the focus of each person's prayers in meditation or petition. As you reflect upon the headline, think about the people and communities affected, the human costs lying behind the newspaper report, its implications for the Christian community, how you and your community can help to create change in the world. (This activity can be done alone as part of one's daily prayers or as part of a group dynamic.) ➤

To have and to have not

Unequal access to goods, services and opportunities is a major problem for millions of people around the world. This exercise will help to start people thinking about this reality, and how they would react if subjected to such inequalities. The group will divide into smaller groups of three to five participants and each small group will be asked to build a mobile (suspended art construction with free-moving parts). Each small group is given a packet which they are told contains all the materials needed for constructing their mobile — paper in different colors, scissors, glue, string, wooden rods, decorations. The groups are told to work with the materials provided in the packet, and the groups not completing the mobile in the designated time will be considered "losers". However, only one packet of materials is complete, and the other packets are each missing some crucial material such as scissors or glue, or have less paper than is needed. Give the groups time to begin their construction, and for them to figure out that their group does not have what it needs to complete the assignment. After the allotted time has run out, let the groups discuss the process. How did they feel when they realized their packet was not complete? How did they feel about the group that had all the materials for the mobile? How did they decide to obtain what they needed to complete the mobile? Now talk about the world we live in. What about those groups within our society that are not given all they need to live their lives? How can we better understand how they feel when they compare themselves with the more affluent in our society? How can we help to create a society that does provide more equitable access for those usually left out because of race, gender, social class, religious beliefs?

NOTES

[1] Dennis A. Jacobsen, Doing Justice, Congregations and Community Organizing, Minneapolis, Fortress, 2001, p. 94.

[2] Jacobsen, p. 95.

[3] Jon Sobrino, "Redeeming Globalization through its Victims," in Concilium, no. 5, 2001, Jon Sobrino and Felix Wilfred eds, Globalization and Its Victims, London, SCM Press, 2001, p. 111.

[4] William Schweiker, "Responsibility in the World of Mammmon," in Religion and Globalization, vol. 1, Max Stackhouse and Peter Paris eds, Harrisburg, Trinity Press, 2000, p. 132.

[5] Schweiker, p. 133.

Isaiah 58:1-11, Matthew 5-7, Letter of James Inés Simeone

The first Christian communities lived in a world dominated by the Roman Empire. They were all trying to fulfil the mission to preach the Gospel of Christ, which for many of them meant working on the margins and opposing the existing system.

It is fairly well known that Rome tried to dominate – and to find "peace" – through the unconditional obedience of its subjects, the recognition of Roman sovereignty, and the absolute authority of the emperor – lord and "master" (over life and death) of all. It is said that there was a common market for all the produce of the earth, which evidently benefited Rome with the best quality products. They say that Rabbi Johuda admired the Romans' achievements: "*How great are the achievements of this nation, they build markets, bridges, baths…!*" To this Rabbi Simon responded: "*Everything that they build is done for their own benefit : they build markets for their prostitutes, baths for their own pleasure and bridges so they can put checkpoints and customs points on them…* [1]» The famous "peace" so highly praised in the Empire, was obviously the result of submission, and payment of taxes and duties etc. Those who disobeyed the established order often paid with death or exile.

Jesus overturned the ideas of the system in place at that moment in history. The Kingdom of God, where there is full life for all, is a contrast to Roman "peace". He came to bring PEACE and the good news of a life of plenty for all. He included those who were marginalized, unprotected or abandoned, giving them the basic hope to stand up and promote change.

It was in these Romanised circumstances, with the great challenge to **preach and live out the Good News** of Jesus Christ, that the first Christian communities, their actions and expressions, came about. Among them were the one in James's letter, to the scattered Jews, and the one in the gospel of Matthew, probably written within a Judaeo-Christian community.

In the well-known Sermon on the Mount (Matt. 5:1-7:29), Matthew presents a series of Jesus's teachings on the true values of the Kingdom of God, living in the light of the Gospel. James, in his letter, presents a collection of teachings on various practical aspects of Christian life.

Both Matthew and James write about the need to put the message received into practice, (Jam. 1:22-27); the affirmation of true faith involving a commitment, firm and solid construction, and consistent practice (Matt. 7:24-29); not discriminating against anybody (Jam. 2:1-9); faith that is shown in works (Jam. 2:14-26); the need for more than words in order to enter the Kingdom of God (Matt. 7:15-23); true wisdom (Jam. 3:13-18); caring for community relations (Jam. 4:11-12); not taking pride in plans (Jam. 4:13-17); waiting patiently and remaining firm in the Lord (Jam. 5:7-8).

These messages call on us to think about our actions, to resist, overturn, convert and transform the values imposed by the ruling system when these go against the values taught by Christianity.

Many Christians in the first communities were believable because they embodied, lived, served, and resisted for their beliefs, for what they preached. Many people gave their lives for it.

There are probably parallels to be drawn with the world of the first believers. Today we live in a globalized world, dominated by other empires. This globalization offers many benefits but at the same time leads to injustices, inequalities, frustrations, exclusions etc. The benefits are only reaped by a minority of the people who (through education, opportunity, geography or choice) accept, obey and get involved in the system. The rest remain largely excluded from the benefits even though they work so that others may enjoy them (and often not even this).

How can we be a Christian community – inheritors of Jesus' teachings and the practices of the first Christians – in today's world? How can we do it if it means being excluded from the system? How can we oppose all that brings death and proclaim abundant life, as Jesus taught?

The answers have to come from within each community, but it is important to highlight the passage in Isaiah which, from another time and place, is still relevant as it invites us to look closely at religious practices, recognise faults, repent, commit and submit to building a community which is just, charitable and peaceful.

> …Is not this the fast that I choose: to loose the bonds of injustice, to undo the thongs of the yoke, to let the oppressed go free, and to break every yoke? Is it not to share your bread with the hungry, and bring the homeless poor into your house; when you see the naked, to cover them, and not to hide yourself from your own kin? Then your light shall break forth like the dawn, and your healing shall spring up quickly... (Isa. 58:6-8)

Today's Christian communities need to look at themselves, analyse and evaluate themselves, change and try to bring about internal and external "healing". This is fundamental in order to continue being living witnesses to the message of life that the Lord gave us.

For this "healing" it is crucial to: resist temptations (such as consumerism, success through the "failure" of others, individualism or competition); recognise the injustices committed; repent; forgive; accept difference and people who are different; exercise humility, commit to the embodiment of the Gospel; develop mutual trust; integrate in spite of disharmony; live in LOVE and make true ecumenism a reality.

This is why we ask, like the song: Breathe, breathe strongly, Spirit of God, come to us with strength, plant your seed of abundant life and make it grow in all of creation... breathe, breathe strongly, Spirit of God. Move us with fire and passion, giving us the courage to shout out the Word of Life which inspires action. Breathe, breath strongly, Spirit of God. Make the gift of love bloom, the gift which when fruitful brings justice and leads to peace and communion within us. (song by Inés Simeone and Horacio Vivares)

How can Christian communities in a globalized world resist and heal?

This question needs real and deep thought from the community. In the light of the texts in Isaiah 58:1-11, Matthew 5-7 and James's letter, look at our current actions, evaluate them and change those tendencies for future actions of resistance and healing.

This challenge can be worked on during a community meeting day (or over several meetings) divided into separate time slots within the same space. Children, teenagers, young people and adults (men and women of all ages) can be involved in this.

1.   *"The Spirit breathes", see and feel the reality*

What was it like at the time of the first communities? (Ask one person or group in the community to research and speak about life under the rule of the Roman Empire)

What is it like now? (To know what it is like today look at the globalized world from a worldwide, national and local perspective. This could be prepared in advance by the groups looking into the situation).

The groups or individuals should present their findings about life then and now in a creative manner (models, photographs, drama). End the session with a song and a prayer.

2.   *"The Spirit breathes", travel in time, understand the message of the prophet Isaiah, Matthew and James*

Work in groups on the selected passages. Each group should try to understand the message, trying to put themselves in the place (in time and space) of that community and answer the following: How is the message of the text a reaction to or resistance of the circumstances the community was living in? Are there any signs that they looked for alternative solutions?

The groups' answers can be shared in a poster (with collages or paintings etc.) a news bulletin, a role play, with a song of thanksgiving in between each presentation. Summarise the similarities.

3.   *"The Spirit breathes", inspires and challenges us to change!*

Taking inspiration from these activities, in new groups answer the following questions: What are the challenges of today's globalized world? How do we behave as communities, as Christians, in the face of reality? What do we have to do to be a BODY which is harmonious, healthy, consistent and practising

Christ's message? How can we go about building a community (local, national or world-wide) that is just, charitable and peaceful?

Share each group's discussions and prepare something to challenge other groups and communities with.

——

NOTE
[1] Wengst, Klaus, Pax Romana, Paulinas, 1991.

Luke 10:25-37   Johannes Nissen

Healing, reconciliation and mission in a broken world

Just then a lawyer stood up to test Jesus. "Teacher," he said, "what must I do to inherit eternal life?" He said to him, "What is written in the law? What do you read there?" He answered, "You shall love the Lord your God with all your heart, and with all your soul, and with all your strength, and with all your mind; and your neighbour as yourself." And he said to him, "You have given the right answer ; do this, and you will live". But wanting to justify himself, he asked Jesus, "And who is my neighbour?" Jesus replied, "A man was going down from Jerusalem to Jericho, and fell into the hands of robbers, who stripped him, beat him, and went away, leaving him half dead. Now by chance a priest was going down that road; and when he saw him, he passed by on the other side. So likewise a Levite, when he came to the place and saw him, passed by on the other side. But a Samaritan while travelling came near him; and when he saw him, he was moved with pity. He went to him and bandaged his wounds, having poured oil and wine on them. Then he put him on his own animal, brought him to an inn, and took care of him. The next day he took out two denarii, gave them to the innkeeper, and said, 'Take care of him; and when I come back, I will repay you whatever more you spend.' He said, "The one who showed him mercy." Jesus said to him, "Go and do likewise".

The aim of this Bible study is to reflect on healing, reconciliation and mission in a broken world. Its main focus will be on the famous story of the Good Samaritan in Luke 10:25-37. As with many other famous texts, this message has often been tamed.

However, this story has a number of shocking points that might be of relevance for our reflections. Let us look at some of these points.

Redefinition of "neighbourhood"

The parable does not answer the original inquiry of the lawyer. "Who is my neighbour?" The text (10:29) poses the question in insider/outsider terms. However, in the parable, "neighbour" shifts from the object of love to the subject who shows love : "Which of the three, do you think, was a ncighbour to the man... ?" (10:36) The question is turned around in a way that erases boundaries.

Openness to the world of "the other"

The lawyer´s initial question is answered from the point of view of the other – the man lying by the roadside, the person in need of a neighbour. We have to practice our healing and reconciling work from where "the other" actually is. The "other" is here the victim of robbery. This confronts us with the call to serve people in their specific social and historical situations. Otherwise, the Christian community will fail in its calling to be a healing and reconciled community.

A de-centring of perspective

Jesus dares to make a Samaritan the hero of the story; the enemy is placed in the position of the elect and becomes the example for the community. A Jewish audience would have been shocked at holding up a Samaritan as an exemplar while discrediting the respected temple priest and Levite. The shock of reversal in this parable is similar to the foot-washing in John 13. Instead of defining love conceptually, these two stories portray love in dramatic and disturbing action. When a national enemy is given the heroic role and the host at table puts himself in the role of a slave, our usual way of perceiving the world is turned upside down.

Other gospel stories are marked by a similar de-centring of perspective. The disadvantaged – the women, the poor person, the stranger etc. – suddenly take centre stage. A "sinful woman" (Luke 7:36-50), a poor widow (Luke 21:1-4), a tax collector (Luke 19:1-10) and an outsider (Luke 10:30-37) become bearers of God's own good news.

Healing of individuals – reconciliation of groups

The parable of the Good Samaritan is about healing. In the first place, the healing act is directed towards an individual. However, there is also another aspect of the story. The parable must be seen in the light of the hate and conflict between Jews and Samaritans at the time of Jesus. Compare this parable to other stories about Samaritans: John 4:1-42; Luke 9:51-56. We are invited to the task of repairing broken relationships between two particular groups.

Luke 10:25-37 is often considered to be the biblical justification of charity work, but it is more than this. The Samaritan does not perform a simple, charitable action. Rather, he enacts what we might call "liberative action"; that is, a combination of aid and a kind of help which makes it possible for the man who was fallen into the hands of robbers to walk again by himself. Samaritan diakonia, or service to others, is an option for life; it is a support for those who have fallen and lie half-dead by the roadside of history, so that they may be liberated and be able to enjoy life in its fullness, the abundant life which comes from God.

Seeing – having compassion – acting

In what way does the Samaritan react to the man fallen into the hands of robbers? He "saw him", "he was moved with pity" and "he went to him" (10:33-34). All three steps are important. First, it is impossible to help without first *seeing* those in need. We are not able to detect those who suffer just by studying statistics or by reading reports. They are real persons in flesh and blood. Therefore, it is indispensable to see. Second, we are told that the Samaritan was moved by *pity* (10:33). However, the word "pity" is a pallid translation of the original Greek (*esplangchnisthe*) that means being shaken in the depths of the womb. Compassion goes beyond pity; it bridges the gap between perception and effective action. This brings us to the third point: The Samaritan "went to him". It is only when all three actions have been taken that the Samaritan can do what is required.

It should be noticed that Jesus´ healing ministry is sometimes described as "compassion". One example is Matthew 9:35-38: "When he saw the crowds, he had compassion for them, because they were harassed and helpless, like sheep without a shepherd" (9:36). Jesus´ compassion is not just a sentimental attitude of concern, but one that results from personal contact with the poor and the oppressed. His compassion functions as social awareness and is translated into mission (compare Matthew 10:1-16). We need to see people in need in order to be shaken from our complacency. We need to learn to see the crowds as Jesus saw them – with eyes of compassion. Indifference and apathy have no place in the Christian life

The divine love

The Samaritan has often been interpreted as a symbol of Christ. He has been seen as the good shepherd (John 10). This interpretation is supported by the fact that Jesus is called "Samaritan" in John 8:48. Perhaps more interesting is another resemblance between Jesus and the Samaritan. On his way to Jericho, Jesus met a blind beggar who shouted "Jesus, Son of David, have mercy on me!" Jesus stood still – and healed the man (Luke 18,35-43). Similarly, the Samaritan did not pass by on that same road, but stopped, thereby indicating that divine love is always on the alert. It can never be postponed.

For further reflection

This parable illustrates that the imagination is invited to move from the pattern of Jesus´ story to discover how to act faithfully in a new situation. The final statement is "Go and do likewise" (10:37). The mandate is not "Go and do exactly the same" as the Samaritan did in the story. It is decidedly not "Go and do whatever you want". The term "likewise" implies that Christians should be faithful to the story of Jesus, yet creative in applying it to their own contexts and the specific needs of those around them. How, then, are we faithfully to apply the text?

The *"Good Muslim"*. In this story Jesus challenged the expectations of the Jewish audience by pointing to a Samaritan as an example. Today, a similar reversal of expectations might occur if we were to combine the notion of compassion with the notion of a foreigner or another person we dislike. In Western countries an increasing number of doctors and social workers from other lands, or proclaiming alternate lifestyles, are working at hospitals, homes for the elderly etc. Some people are not happy to receive assistance from these "others". Even outside the West, clashes in world culture lead to a temptation to raise barriers between communities.

How should the church react to this phenomenon? Does it make sense to speak of "The Good Muslim", or "The Good Homosexual"? Would people in a culture mistrustful of the United States be impressed by a parable of "The Good American"? If these examples are found to be irrelevant, do you have other suggestions?

Blindness versus perception. The priest and the Levite notice the beaten, stripped man but keep their distance in order to avoid any contact that might defile them. He might be a gentile or even a corpse. In this sense, he is "untouchable". They cannot afford to perceive his full humanity because his condition is threatening.

What kind of people are considered to be untouchable in your society? How do you look at persons who suffer from HIV and AIDS?

The interpretive role of outsiders. Christian interpretation of Scripture is enriched by the encounter with outsiders. In Luke 24:13-35 a stranger (Jesus) enables the Emmaus disciples to see in a new way. The importance of the outsider is also underlined in Matthew 15:21-28 (the Cannaanite woman) and by Acts 10:1-11:18 (Peter and Cornelius). The last story emphasizes the role of the Holy Spirit in bridging ancient divisions.

How do you listen to the voices of outsiders in your own context?

Mission as reconciliation – an embracing of the other. The gospel of Jesus Christ is essentially "stranger"-centred. Christian faith is based on the commitment to embrace and accept the other person in his or her otherness. "The church is called to be a healing community and an open and secure space for vulnerable people" (CWME Prepatory Paper No. 3). The image of the Good Samaritan, if internalized as a model, may lead one to a general perspective from which one sees all humankind as a single family under God, and it might evoke the specific intention of helping to break down barriers that in fact still separate "Jew" and "Samaritan", male and female, bond and free (Gal 3:28).

Who are the "others" in your community? In what way can the parable in Luke 10 illustrate this call to be reconciled communities?

Seeing the world "from below". The challenge is to see the world from the viewpoint of the victims, from the viewpoint of the poor and little ones. "Little ones", in the strategy of Jesus, became not only the objects but also the subjects of mission. To think of the implications of taking seriously this understanding of mission is mind-boggling.

Can a church of the "great ones", the "strong ones", the "prosperous ones" or the "comfortable ones" evangelize or be evangelized by the "little ones" of this earth? Who are the little ones in your society? What are we doing for them, and what is their place as facilitators of mission and servants of the gospel through our churches?

Theory and practice – the integrity of mission. "You have given the right answer. Do this and you will live" (Luke 10:29). The lawyer knows what to do. Can he put it into practice? Integrity of mission is holistic – witnessing through words, through works and through transformed lives.

How can this integrity of mission be made real in your own life?

James 5:13-18 James Poling

---

*A*re any among you suffering? They should pray. Are any cheerful? They should sing songs of praise. Are any among you sick ? They should call for the elders of the church and have them pray over them, anointing them with oil in the name of the Lord. The prayer of faith will save the sick, and the Lord will raise them up; and anyone who has committed sins will be forgiven. Therefore confess your sins to one another, and pray for one another, so that you may be healed. The prayer of the righteous is powerful and effective. Elijah was a human being like us, and he prayed fervently that it might not rain, and for three years and six months id did not rain on the earth. Then he prayed again, and the heaven gave rain and the earth yielded its harvest.

Anointing those in need of healing

When I was a child, James 5:13-18 was one of the favorite scriptures in my Christian community. From time to time, someone in our congregation had a serious illness and my father, who was a pastor, would lead an anointing service for healing. I remember hearing sermons about this text, hearing reports from my father about his ministry of healing, and several times, and being present for an anointing service. When I became a pastor, I conducted such services for many sick members, including a public Sunday morning anointing service for a young man facing heart surgery. Later, I led several anointing services of healing in the seminary community where I taught. Every time we had such a service, several dozen people would come forward to have oil placed on their forehead while they knelt before the altar of God.

I would place my hands on their head and pray for healing for their spirits and bodies. Two years ago, my brother led an anointing service for my father as he lay dying in the hospital. It gave all of us a sense of peace about his life and ministry and our relationships with one another. Participating in anointing for healing has always been a moving ritual for me.

I was surprised when I first became active in ecumenical settings and discovered that not all Christians practiced anointing for healing on a regular basis. For some churches anointing with oil evolved into a last rite at the point of death. For others, it became a part of a larger healing ministry focused on prayer and miraculous healing. Until recently, many churches have ignored the healing needs of the community.

Although this specific ritual is not mentioned in Paul or the gospels, James 5:13-18 tells us that the Christians in Jerusalem practiced anointing and prayer for the sick. Apparently the letter of James was written for Jewish Christians who lived all over the Roman Empire, in what is known as the Jewish diaspora (or "dispersion"), to give them courage in the face of persecution. [1] We must remember that during the first centuries prayer was one of the only effective responses to serious illness and injuries from violence.

This text raises two salient issues about healing in an economically globalized world. First, what does it mean to be sick? In the first century, illnesses included physical problems such as fever, bleeding, leprosy, disabilities (blindness, loss of arms or legs), and demon possession. Jesus' healing ministry brought relief to the poor who could not afford to visit the temple doctors. Healing and justice were always interconnected in Jesus' teaching and ministries. Some churches define sickness in narrow physical terms. For example, in my childhood, I only remember anointing services in situations of severe physical illness. Often conducted in a hospital room, the service was used to supplement Western medical treatment. In recent years some churches have begun to explore the relationship of body and spirit. Sometimes a physical ailment can lead to mental or spiritual distress. Sometimes a mental or spiritual ailment can lead to physical illness.

In my more recent ministry, I have offered anointing services for survivors of violence who have struggled for many years with post-traumatic stress disorders. Symptoms such as physical illnesses, depression, anxiety and other complex body-mind experiences require the prayers of the church. We need to be sensitive to the wide experiences of people who come to the church for healing, rather than ignoring the needs of those who do not fit our definitions of physical illness. In my imagination, I wonder about other areas of brokenness in our world, such as conflict between nations, economic exploitation of the poor through corporate greed, and destruction of the environment by modern technology. How do we pray for healing for these areas of community and sickness?

Second, what do we mean by healing? The text says: "The prayer of faith will save the sick, and the Lord will raise them up, and anyone who has committed sins will be forgiven."[2] Many Christians believe in miraculous healing and attend services where healing regularly occurs. Praying fervently in faith in the name of Jesus Christ is a powerful ritual for believers, and healing results often follow. But prayers for healing are not always answered the way Christians expect. For example, when we anointed my father and prayed over him, we wanted him to live. When he died, we realized that healing for our family involved more than physical cure; it also involved spiritual comfort and the healing of relationships.

Mature Christians must have a broad understanding of healing. The human brokenness of body, mind and soul within the world is a complex reality, and prayer helps us see this reality from the perspective of God. On one hand, faithful people believe Jesus' words, "Ask and it will be given to you" (Mt 7:7; Lk 11:19). We come to God in faith, trusting that God will respond to us in love and that our prayers will be answered. On the other hand, our human expectations can get in the way of what God is doing in our lives. When we have definite expectations of what God must do, we can feel that our prayers go unanswered. It is better, in faith, to seek God's righteousness alone; then, the things we truly need will follow (Mt 6:33).

When we gather for prayers and anointing for healing in today's world, what should we pray for? We can gather for prayers for physical healing for those who have diseases such as HIV/AIDS. We can gather for prayers for emotional healing for survivors of violence who live in fear that the trauma will soon return. Can we also gather for prayers for healing among the nations who seek to dominate one another? Can we gather for prayers for healing for corporations that deprive the poor of land and food? Can we gather for prayers for healing for children who carry guns in the large cities of every nation?

James 5:13-18 provides a starting point for us to look at the deeper needs for the healing of individuals, families, churches, nations and the environment. Perhaps we can reinstitute healing services in a much broader context than before, and thus expand our awareness to the broadest kind of healing available: the healing that God offers to all humankind in the name of Jesus Christ.

Methodology

1. Opening prayer
2. Read the passage from James aloud: It is good if members of the class can take a turn in reading, or if everyone can read together
3. Give a short introduction of the historical context. James is a book of wisdom intended for Jewish Christians in the diaspora. It was intended to be a guide to theology and practices. In this verse we have a reminder for Christians to practice a specific healing ritual of anointing with oil. What kind of health care system did they have at that time? What might prayers for healing have meant for them during a time of persecution?
4. List potential illnesses appropriate for healing service. What kind of healing services are practiced in your communities? What new forms of healing services could be added to services for healing that you already practice?

Usual understanding of healing	Expanded understanding of healing

➤

5. Brainstorm on how the service of anointing for healing might be adapted for expanded understandings of healing. Where would it take place? Who would participate? Who would officiate? Who or what would be anointed? What kinds of prayers could be said?
6. What are the possible results from a healing service? What kinds of expectations are appropriate for Christian prayer?
7. Closing Prayer

NOTES

[1] Richard Bauckham, *James*, London, Routledge, 1999, p.25.

[2] All references are from the *New Revised Standard Bible in English*, Zondervan, 1989.

5 *Proclaiming Hope*

2 Corinthians 5:11-21   Moon-Geoung Kim

*T*herefore, knowing the fear of the Lord, we try to persuade others; but we ourselves are well known to God, and I hope that we are also well known to your consciences. We are not commending ourselves to you again, but giving you an opportunity to boast about us, so that you may be able to answer those who boast in outward appearance and not in the heart. For if we are beside ourselves, it is for God; if we are in our right mind, it is for you. For the love of Christ urges us on, because we are convinced that one has died for all; therefore all have died. And he died for all, so that those who live might no longer live for themselves, but for him who died and was raised for them. From now on, therefore, we regard no one from a human point of view; even though we once knew Christ from a human point of view, we know him no longer in that way. So if anyone is in Christ, there is a new creation: everything old has passed away; see, everything has become new! All this is from God, who reconciled us to himself through Christ, and has given us the ministry of reconciliation; that is, in Christ God was reconciling the world to himself, not counting their trespasses against them, and entrusting the message of reconciliation to us. So we are ambassadors for Christ, since God is making his appeal through us; we entreat you on behalf of Christ, be reconciled to God. For our sake he made him to be sin who knew no sin, so that in him we might become the righteousness of God.

What the text says

This text, 2 Corinthians 5:11-21, is about the reconciliation with God accomplished in Jesus Christ, which serves as the hope which the faithful proclaim. The text can be divided for study into three parts: 1. verses 11-13: how Paul serves; 2. verses 14-17: how the love of Christ is the basis for the apostle's service; 3. verses 18-21: how the faithful serve.

1. Verses 11-13

It is Paul's knowledge of the Lord which defines his service as an apostle. Only because he fears the Lord does Paul try, as a witness, to persuade people and win them over to God, not for his own benefit (verse 11). Paul wants to give the church in Corinth reason to rejoice in their apostle and to show their loyalty to him with conviction, over against those who are working against Paul in the Corinthian churches (verse 12). Paul's efforts in every situation are for God alone, and it is in this sense that he is thinking and working to build up the church. Love for God and care for the church, these are the two poles which govern the apostle's service (verse 13).

2. Verses 14-17

The governing principle for the apostle Paul, and for Christians in every age, is the love of Christ, which is revealed in his suffering and death on our behalf (verse 14). The atoning death of Jesus Christ opens the way to new, eternal life. The faithful no longer live for themselves, but rather for him who died for them and was raised again. The power of Jesus Christ's resurrection gives the new and genuine chance to live (verse 15). Through Christ's act of love on the cross Paul overcomes the knowledge of Christ "from a human point of view". The encounter with Christ leads to a new, "spiritual" way of knowing. A person who lives for Christ sees every person through the eyes of Jesus Christ, as someone whom Christ loves and redeems, someone for whom Christ died (verse 16). Through the death of Jesus Christ, what is old has passed away. Through his resurrection, new life is present. When the faithful no longer live for themselves but for Christ and the people around them, their sisters and brothers, there is truly new life. The eschatological hope for a new creation has now been accomplished in Jesus Christ (verse 17).

3. Verses 18-21

Because of sin, "wanting to be like God", human beings and the world live at enmity with God. But this enmity is overcome, "from God's side". God's action of reconciliation is accomplished through the cross and resurrection of his son Jesus Christ. *The rec-*

onciliation which has taken place must be proclaimed as the living hope for humankind and the world. It is God who performed the service of reconciliation for us, through Christ (verse 18). It is God who accomplished the reconciliation with the world, in Jesus Christ. The apostle, and the faithful of every age, have the mission to continue proclaiming this message of reconciliation (verse 19). The word of God, of reconciliation in Christ, is given by God to preachers to deliver. For Christ's sake, the apostle and the faithful serve as messengers of God's act of reconciliation. For Christ's sake, they call upon others to be reconciled with God (verse 20). Jesus Christ endured death for our sake, for the sake of our sins, to call us out of our death in sin into "life in Christ". Thus God makes us righteous in Jesus Christ. He becomes our sins, and only in Jesus Christ will we experience God's righteousness. When the faithful allow themselves to be seized by this reconciliation with God, they live as justified persons (verse 21).

Instructions for Bible study

All participants should read the text and reflect upon it. To make practical use of the message of the text, the leader can ask the participants the following five questions. The additions to the questions can be brought in as aids to the questions. All participants should share their own reflexions and experiences with one another. At the end of the study, all participants should pray together in the name of the Holy Spirit.

Questions on the Bible study

1. What is the purpose of my service to my church congregation? (verses 11-13)
- for God or for myself? (verses 11 and 13)
- for my own inner certainty or for an outward appearance? (verse 12)

2. How do I know Jesus Christ, myself and other people? (verses 14-17)
- according to "a human point of view" or according to "the Spirit"? (verse 16)

➤

3. What is "reconciliation" according to the Bible, and how does it take place? (verses 18-21)
- - who is at work? (verses 18-19)
- what is the basis of reconciliation? (verse 21)
- why do we need this reconciliation? (verse 21)

4. With whom should I be reconciled, and how? (verses 18-21)
- with God in Jesus Christ?
- with myself?
- with other people around me (concretely) and the world?

5. What should my service be? (verses 18-21)
- to what am I called?
- am I to proclaim reconciliation with God in Jesus Christ? (verses 20-21)

Revelation 21:1-11; and 21:22 – 22:5

V. Rocha

People with a prophetic vision of a new world[1]

*T*hen I saw a new heaven and a new earth; for the first heaven and the first earth had passed away, and the sea was no more. And I saw the holy city, the new Jerusalem, coming down out of heaven from God, prepared as a bride adorned for her husband. And I heard a loud voice from the throne saying, "See, the home of God is among mortals. He will dwell with them as their God; they will be his peoples, and god himself will be with them; he will wipe every tear from their eyes. Death will be no more; mourning and crying and pain will be nor more, for the first things have passed away." And the one who was seated on the throne said, "See, I am making all things new." also he said, "Write this, for these words are trustworthy and true." Then he said to me, "It is done! I am the Alpha and the Omega, the beginning and the end. To the thirsty I will give water as a fight from the spring of the water of life. Those who conquer will inherit these things, and I will be their God and they will be my children. But as for the cowardly, the faithless, the polluted, the murderes, the fornicators, the sorcerers, the idolaters, and all liars, their place will be in the lake that burns with fire and sulfur, which is the second death." Then one of the seven angels who had the seven bowls full of the seven last plagues came and said to me, "Come, I will show you the bride, the wife of the Lamb." And in the spirit he carried me away to a great, high mountain and showed me the holy city Jerusalem coming down out of heaven from God. It has the glory of God and a radiance like a very rare jewel, like jasper, clear as crystal. (...)
I saw no temple in the city, for its temple is the Lord god the Almighty and the Lamb. And the city has no need of sun or moon

to shine on it, for the glory of God is its light, and its lamp is the Lamb. The nations will walk by its light, and the kings of the earth will bring their glory into it. Its gates will never be shut by day – and there will be no night there. People will bring into it the glory and the honor of the nations. But nothing unclean will enter it, nor anyone who practices abomination or falsehood, but only those who are written in the Lamb's book of life. (...)
Then the angel showed me the river of the water of life, bright as crystal, flowing from the throne of God and of the Lamb through the middle of the street of the city. On either side of the river, is the tree of life with its twelve kinds of fruit, producing its fruit each month; and the leaves of the tree are for the healing of the nations. Nothing accursed will be found there any more. But the throne of God and of the Lamb will be in it, and his servants will worship him; they will see his face, and his name will be on their foreheads. And there will be no more night; they need no light of lamp or sun, for the Lord God will be their light, and they will reign forever and ever.

Readers of the Bible can have different reactions to the Book of Revelation to John. Out of my experience as a woman who is a believer and who has hope, this book is a treasure house of possibilities in the midst of impossibilities. These biblical texts invite us to approach everyday situations, not as set solutions or lists of instructions, but as a challenge to our minds and the practice of our faith.

The contrast between the new and the old is present all through the biblical story, and this same tension is experienced daily in the communities that, in their many differing ways, show signs of resistance and the desire to build something new.

A new order of creation

The advent of this new world is described as something visible: no more tears, no more death, no more mourning, no more crying, no more pain, no more of the former world. All these words seem to imply the same thing: that there will be no more suffering. The list becomes longer in vv. 23 and 25: there is no more sun, no more night. The reason for this is given in v. 5: "Behold, I make all things new!" It is a robust affirmation: "These words are trustworthy and true."

The symbols used to describe this new order are varied and very close to people's lives: bride, wedding, temple, clothes, water of life. In the symbolism of the wedding a prominent feature is happiness. All sorts of preparations have to be made for the happiness that people will share in the celebrations, for this moment of here and now. It is a moment given by God for people to relax together and celebrate the beauty and greatness of life, at a place and time when relationships can be formed and strengthened. This new creation includes Jerusalem coming down from heaven. The city has distinctive attributes: it is resplendent (v. 11) and as clear as crystal. The structure and form of the city indicate its perfection. It is cosmopolitan, with a strong sense of including the whole inhabited earth (oikoumene). It is the city where God dwells and the nations live in the light of the glory of God. This new city seems to include the two traditional opposites of both town and country. The city seems to become the one and only place, with an open door policy, its gates always open to the various nations.[2] The Lord God and the Lamb are its temple, and there is no longer any division between the levels of heaven and earth, the sacred and the profane.

Nature itself is part of this city and not its enemy. The angel shows John a river of the water of life flowing from the throne of God and of the Lamb. The vision is completed with the tree of life, which is reminiscent of the Garden of Eden in Genesis. This reference to the beginning shows us that there will no longer be any curse, which is a total reversal of Genesis 3:17. The city and its inhabitants will reign with God for ever and ever.

Symbols as aids to learning

Symbols can also be tools for learning. The Book of Revelation points to a learning method consisting of seeing/writing/discerning and nourishing hope.[3] Building hope is not only a matter of faith, but also involves strategy, struggle and experience. The prophetic vision presented to us in these texts is a message in language which re-expresses the utopia of a new world, or a new cosmos, in which reconciliation is possible at all levels of human life and its surroundings. The language of Revelation has as its aim the empowerment of its readers so that the vision becomes a concrete, real possibility. The symbols are forceful, powerful, inspiring people to take action accompanied by God's grace. They are prophetic visions to reaffirm the need for reconciliation and healing for men and women, nations and the world itself.

These biblical texts are an affirmation that another world is possible, in which life in abundance becomes evident, and also the values of justice, peace and equality enable relations to be established across frontiers, differences, powers and narrowness of mind. Finally, the beginning of the Book of Revelation reminds us: "Let those who have ears hear what the Spirit is saying..."

Something to think about

1. How do you react when you read these passages?
2. What phrase do you find most inspiring in these passages?

Something to do

1. Individually, draw a symbol of the present world order in which we are living, name it and place it in the centre of the room.
2. Together, draw symbols of the new world order of which we dream, name them, and, using your imagination, place them alongside the symbols of "the past".

Something to celebrate

We sing: Ale, ale, alleluia!

An act of commitment

Lord, inspire us with visions and dreams.
Challenge us with your truth.
Empower us with your strength,
To build that different world.

Lord, inspire us to keep hope alive,
And the capacity to dream.
We commit ourselves to listen to your voice,
Even in the midst of despair.

Lord, we commit ourselves
To see, to listen and to speak,
In full awareness that, if we fail to do so,
The stones will have to do it.
We commit ourselves to persevere in celebrating
In advance this new creation,
Affirming that your promises hold good
Now and for ever. Amen.

NOTES

¹ I prefer to use the term 'prophetic' because of the sense of militant action it contains, in relation to both individual and collective initiatives, which encourages us to continue struggling for a just and peaceful world order, inspired by our faith and hope in the God of Life.

² In contrast to a globalization that implies uniformity, this vision reaffirms a community of peoples and nations, living together illumined by justice and peace.

³ Rather than being a mysterious, strange, complicated or terrifying book, the Book of Revelation can offer us an alternative, critical interpretation, involving an educational process of learning and unlearning.

Matthew 8:15   Keith Warrington

*H*e *(Jesus) touched her hand, and the fever left her, and she rose and served him.*

This healing of Peter's mother-in-law by Jesus is recorded in each of the Synoptic gospels (Matthew, Mark and Luke) and each says that Jesus touched her. In healing people, Jesus often used his hands (Matt. 8:3,15; 9:29; 17:7; 20:34; Mark 5:41; 7:33; 10:46-52; 9:29; Luke 7:14; 13:13; 22:51; John 9:6), and this is significant for a number of reasons:

A sign of compassion

The element of compassion was undoubtedly an important aspect in the use of touch (Matt. 14:14; 20:34; Mark 1:41; 5:19; Luke 7:13), though it was not the prime motivation in the healings of Jesus. Matthew refers to it in only two cases (14:14 and 20:34); Mark, possibly, once (1:41); Luke, once (7:13); and John, never. If it could be shown that compassion was the major motive for Jesus' ministry of healing, or even a significantly important one, it would be appropriate to ask why Jesus did not heal all the sick in the region. In John 5:3-5, Jesus chose not to heal all, but only one. Other reasons are identified by the authors of the gospels to indicate his uniquely exalted nature and mission.

Nevertheless, to receive a touch from a fellow member of humanity, let alone from one who bore the hallmarks of being God himself, provided a powerful message to the sick. Generally, the perception of the people was that the gods were uncaring; the unfulfilled desire of many was for a benevolent deity. Jesus Christ provided such a deity. Luke (18:15) particularly demonstrates this feature when he recalls Jesus touching children who came to him. However, although this account is also recorded in Matthew and Mark, Luke informs his readers that Jesus touches babies/infants. Jesus is presented as having time, not just for children, but also for those who may be so young that they have no concept of who he is, too young to be able to tell. Jesus is recorded as having time for those who may not be able to respond to him or even know how to respond; this reveals the character of the one who desires to give more than to receive.

A demonstration of the authority of Jesus

The use of hands in healing is more likely to correspond to the authority of Jesus. The general assumption of the Jews was that sickness was the result of the sin of those who were suffering or of their parents (John 9:2). Since God had sanctioned suffering as a punishment for personal sin, it was assumed that only God could remove it. The person concerned was deemed to be ceremonially sick, as demonstrated by his/her sickness. For centuries before the time of Jesus, the Jews had looked forward to an era when sickness would be removed, though the prospect of suffering being removed prior to the end-times was an infrequent hope (1 Enoch 10:10f; 102:4; 104:2). This great hope began to be fulfilled in the ministry of Jesus.

Jesus – who could not be contaminated by sickness, ceremonially or otherwise – touched the sick whilst at the same time transmitting his wholeness to them. Readers were reminded of references in the Hebrew scriptures to the powerful hand/arm of God (Num. 11:23; 1 Sam. 5:7; 1 Chron. 29:12; Job 5:18; Isa. 1:25). The hand of God, according to gospel narratives, is now in evidence in the hand of Jesus. Such a healing practice and the authority vested in it serves to emphasize the authority of Jesus.

A determination to include the marginalized

The fact that Jesus is regularly presented as touching those who are sick indicates a radical departure from normative Jewish practice for in touching those who were ill, Jesus was touching those who were ceremonially unclean. The Jews believed that

God sent sickness to test them or frequently, as a result of their sin, to chastise or discipline them (Gen 32:32; Ex. 15:26; Lev. 26 :14ff; Deut. 7:12ff). Thus, those who were ill were often deemed to be impure (for example, Lev. 13:14), and a stigma was associated with them (Ps. 38:11, 12; John 9:2). To touch those who assumed that the hand of God was against them, as demonstrated in sickness, was a precocious act.

Consequently, people who were ill often led lonely lives. This was due, in part, to their inability to function as normal members of the community in contrast to their able-bodied colleagues. In addition, it was based on a belief that personal sin had caused the illness, the latter having been sent by God as a form of chastisement. Social ostracism often resulted, or at least a form of marginalization from others in the community. If God had punished individuals, it was difficult for the community to be seen to be undermining that divine action by accepting the afflicted persons into society as if nothing had happened to them.

The majority of those healed were drawn from the poor sectors of society, including beggars, women and children; such people could not afford the fees relating to medical care. In healing them, Jesus dissolved the social barriers that separated people from each other and introduced them to the possibility that God was not as far from them as they may have feared.

Matthew records Jesus' healing ministry as being directed to people on the margins of society (8:1-13; 9:1-7, 27-30; 14:14; 15:22) as does Mark, including the healing of non-Jews (7:24-30; 5 :1-20; 7:31-37) and the ritually impure (1:40-45; 5:25-34). Similarly, Luke (4:16-30) records Jesus' sermon in Nazareth in which Jesus declares that he has come to minister to those on the perimeter of society, Jesus being presented as healing gentiles (7:1-10; 17:11-19) and those excluded from society (5:12-16; 8:26-39; 19:1-10).

The significance of this is not simply to illustrate that Jesus had compassion on those rejected by society so much as to demonstrate his authority to incorporate them back into society as fully contributing members, with the new revelation that God had not rejected them, for their illnesses had been removed. In this regard, Jesus is presented as fulfilling the prophecies concerning a new age in which God's mercy would be fully revealed (Isa. 14:1; 49:13; 54:8; 55:3; Jer. 12:15). God, in the person of Jesus, has come to touch hurt humanity and infuse his own wholeness into lives that have been broken and scarred.

Thus, the gospel healings are provided as records of Jesus meeting the marginalized and dispossessed, providing hope for the hopeless and help for the helpless. Through his healings, Jesus offered freedom to those bound by illness or demonic influence, and any attendant societal or religious restrictions, making it possible for them to be reintegrated into society and into their faith community whilst also enabling them to be productive again. Although not all benefited fully from the potential provided by Jesus to actualize their freedom, his healing ministry encapsulates his mission to a humanity in its weakness. This determination to minister to the marginalized, integrating them again into society, must be more frequently reflected in contemporary Christian healing.

"So Ananias departed and entered the house. And laying his hands on him he said, 'Brother Saul, the Lord Jesus who appeared to you on the road by which you came, has sent me that you may regain your sight and be filled with the Holy Spirit.'" (Acts 9:17)]

The use of hands is also a major element in the healing praxis of the apostles (Acts 9:17, 41; 14:3; 19:11; 28:8) as they reflect Jesus in healing activity and methodology. Here, a relatively unknown character is described as also using the laying on of hands to bring healing to the man who will be one of the most significant leaders in the early church.

A number of lessons may be derived from this account:

- Ananias follows the practice of Jesus, as did the apostles; so also may believers today.

- The characteristic of compassion is present in the use of hands laid on a man who has been suddenly and supernaturally blinded, possibly resulting in uncertainty and fear on his part. The friendliness of hands is appropriate in this context, as it is for all believers.

- The element of authority is very significant in the use of hands, as also demonstrated by Jesus. This is not an automatic authority, nor does the use of hands always indicate that restoration will take place. However, Ananias is responding to a commission from Jesus, as emphasized by the reference to the name of Jesus in his statement to Saul. When combined with the person and authority of Jesus, restoration is to be expected and the use of hands in healing and restoration is an appropriate affirmation of that expectation.

Discussion questions

- In what ways do the following stanzas explore the character of God, as revealed in God's capacity to care?

He flung the stars out into space
and everyone went to its place and stayed.
He dropped the oceans in the sea;
the waters flowed obediently.
He tossed the sun and moon up high;
they shone for Him in the darkened sky.
He in His power and in His might
ordered the day to turn to night.

He commanded everything to be right
for He, the Creator, ruled.
He reigned supreme in splendour, awe;
his glory – no one could endure.
The King did as He pleased and more;
the King just spoke the Word and angels in their
glittering hordes
pounced to obey His every word, their King, their Lord.

But he cradles us in His arms;
He joins us in our storm and gently calms our fears.
He steps into our shoes, just where we are;
He shepherds us with tender care,
with fingers, hands,
love beyond compare.
He flung the stars out into space
but He welcomes us with a warm embrace.
He shows us a glimpse of His eternal grace,
to us, members of a fallen race.
When our name He calls
His love is a soft place to fall.
The King has a smile upon His face
for the Shepherd has made us His own.

- What symbols of reconciliation and restoration are particularly appropriate to your culture and Christian context?

➤

- What are the potential benefits and impact to individuals when being touched in the context of community prayer on their behalf?
- Imagine how people felt when Jesus laid his hands on them (Matt. 9:29; Mark 5:4133; Luke 18:15; John 9:6). What thoughts may have gone through the minds of those who watched?
- In what situations may touching another person be inappropriate? What alternative actions could be incorporated to achieve the same symbolic benefit?
- Does the absence of touch indicate a decrease in the potential of supernatural restoration? Provide evidence for your response.

Isaiah 11:1-9   J. Prior

A shoot will spring from the stock of Jesse, a new shoot will grow from his roots. On him will rest the spirit of the Lord, the spirit of wisdom and insight, the spirit of counsel and power, the spirit of knowledge and fear of the Lord: His inspiration will lie in fearing the Lord. His judgement will not be by appearances, His verdict not given on hearsay. He will judge the weak with integrity and give fair sentence for the humblest in the land. He will strike the country with the rod of his mouth and with the breath of his lips bring death to the wicked. Uprightness will be the belt around his waist, and constancy the belt about his hips. The wolf will live with the lamb, the panther lie down with the kid, calf, lion and fat-stock beast together, with a little boy to lead them. The cow and the bear will graze, their young will lie down together. The lion will eat hay like the ox. The infant will play over the den of the adder; the baby will put his hand into the viper's lair. No hurt, no harm will be done on all my holy mountain, for the country will be full of knowledge of the Lord As the waters cover the sea.

Reflection

The threat of annihilation had rolled on for more than a century. Samaria fell to Assyria in BCE 721, Palestine was ravaged in 701, a year before Isaiah fell silent. Jerusalem itself surrendered a century later (597) and the temple and city walls were pulled down within a decade. For forty years the prophet observed the scene (740-700), fully aware of the inevitable destruction. The name of Isaiah's second child sums up the age: *"Speedy-spoil-quick-booty"* (Isa. 8:1-4). Transfixed by God's glory in the

Jerusalem temple, Isaiah is called to be the conscience of the nation. Unclean among an unclean people, he is burnished by the fire of the Holy One (Isa. 6:1-13). The prophet is the measure of our own possibility of seeing, hearing and understanding with the heart, of being touched and healed.

The book begins in the "old" Jerusalem that will be destroyed (Isa. 1-39), passes through the redemptive suffering of the Babylonian exile (Isa. 40-55) and ends back in the promised land with a vision of the New Jerusalem where all the nations of the world will be reconciled with God, with one another and with nature (Isa. 56-66). Indeed, the vision of the New Jerusalem infuses the entire work (eg. Isa. 2:1-5).

Political intrigue, social injustice and cultic syncretism have brought disaster right up to the gates of Jerusalem. The ruling elite must render account. Yet, against all the crushing odds, the "holy" lives in Isaiah and in those who, like him, take the word of God seriously.

In a world of war and rumours of war, can the word of God survive? In a world where to be normal is to threaten mass destruction, where the terrorism of the disenfranchised is crushed by the terrorism of the state, where the political elite has lost all credibility, what power do we give to Isaiah's image that ploughshares be beaten from swords, that state violence and social conflict give way to concern for the exploited poor and the ravaged earth?

Isaiah is a person of faith, the voice of a small group of faith-survivors who refuse to live according to human expediency, moral compromise or the inhuman values of the violent world around them. Throughout "The Book of Emmanuel" (Isa. 6:1-11 :9) Isaiah weaves a key faith-motif: "If you will not take your stand on me you will not stand firm." (Is 7:9). Faith is trust, trust with the heart, a practised trust under whatever pressure. Trust God, not the city's defences (Isa. 7:7-9).

Amidst the harsh grasp of the increasingly militarized state, the prophet's strident voice of accusation against the rulers alternates with the gentle voice of hope for the populace. Isaiah places little hope in the historic kingship, but rather in a return to the very source of the dynasty, to the very roots of the burnt-out stump of David's father (Is 11:1). Back to pre-monarchic Jesse, to begin anew under a new direction.

Only the infusion of the divine force – *"the spirit of the Lord"* (Isa. 11:2) – will enable future leaders to fulfil their mission.

God's people must return to the earliest charismatic tradition pre-dating the monarchy. The spirit-filled Moses is the ideal (Num. 11:17). A spirit of *"wisdom, insight and counsel"* would have freed Kings Ahaz and Hezekiah of their foolish advisers by granting independence of thought and action. A spirit of *"power"* or *"strength"* makes counsel effective while *"fear of the Lord"* would enable the king to take a clear stand.

And not just take a stand but also take sides. With God's spirit, political leadership will administer justice in favour of the weak (Isa. 11:3-5). The measure of leadership is justice for *"the humblest of the land"*, a preferential concern for the landless and the economically insecure. Policies based on integrity rather than hearsay are a condition for a return to paradise. Ecological mal-function is due to social injustice just as perfect justice leads to perfect peace and natural harmony (Isa. 11:6-9). Social transfor-mation will be completed by a transformation of nature.

A new shoot from the apparently burnt-out stump of Jesse and a return to paradise are ultimately attributed to the spirit's gift of *"knowledge of the Lord"* (Isa. 11:9). Where political leader-ship fails to know and understand the Lord, they inevitably cause evil and occasion disaster (see Isa. 1:3; 5:1-13; 6:9-10). In this crisis moment, for the first time in the Hebrew Bible, God speaks of a total transformation of social and natural reality: a peaceable realm of unchecked creativity and benevolence.

Who is the prophetic sign and presence of the longed-for cred-ible leadership in a harmonious world? Where is the evidence of God's compassionate justice and cosmic providence? It is a child, a baby, an infant (Isa. 11:7-8). Children are our future; the least protected and the most vulnerable are our guarantee. Children are the sign of the presence of the Holy One, evidence that a faithful remnant will survive.

And yet, as Daniel Berrigan says: We grow out of childhood into war. We grow out of the God of childhood into homage towards the gods of war. The gods of our adulthood are diplomatic – glib, mendacious, insipid, tedious, mealy-mouthed. Or they are bellicose – truculent, cocksure, grisly, treacherous, callous, ferocious.

And so we ask: Is Isaiah's dream-vision beyond words? And yet, "Without dreams the people perish." (Pr 29:18). The unitive, pristine and tender word-dream of Isaiah becomes real when we receive the spirit of wisdom and insight, counsel and power, knowledge and fear of the Lord.

Personal/group reflection and study

Prayerful reflection in three steps

1. Read through the passage slowly. Remain silent for a while until a particular word or phrase stands out. In a group each person is given an opportunity to say aloud the word or phrase that is most striking to the reader. More than one person may have chosen the same phrase.

2. Read through the passage slowly again. Remain silent for awhile, and then each person who wishes may briefly mention why that particular word or phrase is striking. No long sermon, just a simple sharing.

3. Read through the passage slowly once more. Remain silent for awhile, and then each person who wishes may turn the phrase they have chosen into a short prayer.

Study in context

One or more of the following themes may be shared/studied.

Burnt-out stump

In what ways has the political elite today become a "burnt-out stump" and lost credibility? What would returning to the source (Jesse's root) – going back to original leadership ideals, motives and characteristics – mean in our situation?

What insights on these matters do we gain from this Isaiah passage?

Child

If you have had a child, share your experiences of being pregnant and/or of becoming a parent. What was your child-bearing a sign of?

If somebody has experienced children as an image of hope, of a new beginning, perhaps even of a "resurrection", let them share that experience. ➤

How can children help us to recover our innocence and prepare the land for a new paradise?

How can we read this Isaiah passage when children are not only signs of hope, but also victims and survivors of exploitation (street children, children living with HIV/AIDS, child soldiers, child prostitutes, child labourers)?

Spirit

What spirit seems to influence leadership most? <u>Note</u>: we have leadership in the family, the local community, the church, and the body politic.

Contrast this spirit or style of leadership with the spirit of *"wisdom and insight, counsel and power, knowledge and fear of the Lord"*.

What first steps can we take to move towards a Spirit-filled leadership?

Bible Studies for
Youth and Children

1 *Come, Holy Spirit, Heal and Reconcile!*

John 4:1-42   M. Campbell

This study will introduce the significance of water in faith community. It transcends common forms and functions to gather people of all ages and ethnic orientations in celebrating the many God-given gifts they share, such as: membership in God's family through baptism, hearts overflowing with love and grace to share, the privilege of serving others as Jesus offered to serve the woman at the well and requested that she would do the same.

Introductory Activity:

Preparation and Supplies:
* An activity sheet for each child
* Pencils, crayons or markers

Leader's Notes:

Refer to the water droplet on the activity sheet. Encourage children to make note of people and places that provide water for recreation, cleansing and refreshment in the space provided. Identify ways people gain access to water, for example: from a river or a lake, a well, a pump, a faucet, a fountain or a hose. Refer to the Bible verse at the bottom of the handout as you point out the invitation Jesus made to come to his "water party".

Story Presentation

Read or act out the following story:

*O*ne day Jesus was on a road trip through the country of Samaria. He stopped near a well to rest. When a woman came by to draw water, Jesus asked her to give him a drink. She was surprised to hear his request because people from his country didn't get along with people from her country. They began to talk and soon she discovered who Jesus was! She was surprised to hear some of the things she heard him say! Jesus said, "Everyone who drinks of this water will be thirsty again, but those who drink of the water that I will give them will never be thirsty. The water I will give them will become in them a spring of water gushing up to eternal life." She asked him for the water he was offering. Then, she left her water jar and went back into the city to tell others to come and meet Jesus. They came and many more believed he was the Saviour they had been waiting for. (John 4:1-42)

Interpreting the Story

Complete the following activity as you engage children in a discussion about water.

Pour water from a pitcher high above a cup to create a dramatic sound effect. Fill a cup three-fourths full of water for each child. Use the cup as a visual aid to point out that about 75 % of their bodies are made up of water. Even though a body is packed with bones and muscles, it has gallons of life-giving water flowing through it. To stay healthy, we need to drink at least 4 litres of water to replenish our bodies each day. And, just like in the Bible story, sometimes we need a little help from from others to get the water we need

Discussion Questions

1) One day Jesus was on a road trip and he became thirsty. Who did he ask to give him a drink? What do you know about her?
2) As they talked Jesus told the woman that he had a special kind of water to drink. How did he describe it?

➤

Point out that Jesus offered to fill her heart with God's love, acceptance and forgiveness, and he promised her that it would last forever. He set aside any human reasons why they shouldn't get along and nurtured a "come-as-you-are" friendship, with God's grace flowing freely between them. We still see the same thing happening today as God claims us as God's own and invites us to be active members of God's global family.

Jesus Loves All the Little Children

Preparation and Supplies:

* Four clear cups or plastic glasses
* Substances that produce a variety of different pigments, like: tea, onionskins and other food colorings or edible plant dyes
* A small spoon or paintbrush
* A black or dark permanent marker
* A pitcher of water

Make the following design on each one of the cups. (1) Draw an outline of a person on one side of all 4 cups. (2) Draw a heart on the opposite side of the cups so it is positioned within the outline of the person. (3) Place a cross inside the heart.

Leader's Notes

Perform a science experiment to illustrate that, no matter where we live or what colour our skin, God calls us to gather, in friendship and community, for worship and for service as God's love flows like living water in and through us.

Fill each cup three-quarters full of water. Recognize water to be a symbol of God's love and acceptance. Place a different pigment in each cup. Identify the coloured versions of each outlined design. Note their similarities. Then, combine pigments to make new colours. Add just enough colour to indicate a change, but still retain the outlined design. Record the colours you combine to make new colours.

Summarize the discoveries of your experiment and interpret it to be a concrete demonstration of God's unconditional love for people of all ages and places.

Optional: Sing or say the words to the song "Jesus Loves the Little Children"

"Jesus loves the little children, all the children of the world. Though we come from many lands, Jesus holds us in his hands. Jesus loves the little children of the world."

Waterworks

Supplies:

* An activity sheet for each child
* Pencils, crayons or markers

Leaders Notes

Refer to the Bible verse printed at the bottom of the sheet with the glass on it. Suggest that "living water" is intended to do more than just sit in a cup. Living water isn't really even associated with a cup, at all. It come in a bowl, a font or a pool at baptism. It pours in with a hug and a random or intentional act of kindness. It is meant to gush and flow - in and through us - as God's love inspires us to draw people into community and provide hope and refreshment for tired and weary hearts and minds.

Invite children to make a note of things they might do to share God's refreshing and life-giving love with others as they grow in friendship and community with them.

Close your time together in prayer, thanking God for providing water to refresh our bodies and love to refresh hearts that are thirsty for signs of God's life-living love.

Luke 4:14-21   John C. Thomas

Then Jesus, filled with the power of the Spirit, returned to Galilee, and a report about him spread through all the surrounding country. He began to teach in their synagogues and was praised by everyone. When he came to Nazareth, where he had been brought up, he went to the synagogue on the sabbath day, as was his custom. He stood up to read, and the scroll of the prophet Isaiah was given to him. He unrolled the scroll and found the place where it was written: "The Spirit of the Lord is upon me, because he has anointed me to bring good news to the poor. He has sent me to proclaim release to the captives and recovery of sight to the blind, to let the oppressed go free, to proclaim the year of the Lord's favour." And he rolled up the scroll, gave it back to the attendant, and sat down. The eyes of all in the synagogue were fixed on him. Then he began to say to them, "Today this scripture has been fulfilled in your hearing."

The significance of Luke 4:14-21 for the gospel according to Luke is impossible to overestimate. For, among other things, this text goes some way towards explaining the relationship between Jesus' anointing by the Spirit, his mission and his ministry of healing.

Returning to Galilee from the wilderness temptations and filled with the Holy Spirit, Jesus reads from the Isaiah scroll in a synagogue in Nazareth:

> The Spirit of the Lord is upon me; therefore he has anointed me to preach good news to the poor. He has sent me to preach release for the captives and recovery of sight to the blind, to release the oppressed, to preach the year of the Lord's favor (Luke 4:18-19).

This programmatic text not only sets the agenda for Jesus' ministry as it will unfold within Luke's gospel, but it also contains in embryonic form many important issues to follow in the gospel: issues related to the Spirit, healing and reconciliation. The observations that follow find their foundation in this text.

First, the strategic location of this passage is revealed in part by the fact that there are no miracles attributed to Jesus in Luke's gospel before this passage appears. However, from this point on Jesus' ministry of healing is a regular part of the gospel story. The importance of this statement is further underscored by the fact that portions of Luke 4:18-19 are repeated at various points in Luke's narrative. For example, consider the response to John's question to Jesus, "Are you the coming one or should we expect another?" Jesus, who at the moment when John's disciples arrive to ask the question is involved in healing many from various diseases, illnesses, unclean spirits, and blindness, hearkens back to the words of Isaiah quoted in Luke 4:

> "Go tell John that which you have seen and heard; the blind receive their sight, the lame walk, the lepers are cleansed and the deaf hear, the dead are being raised, and the poor are receiving the good news" (Luke 7:22).

Still later in the gospel, echoes of this activity are heard in Jesus' response to word brought by the Pharisees that Herod was trying to kill him. On this occasion Jesus says:

> "Go tell that fox, 'Behold I cast out demons and accomplish healings today and tomorrow, and on the third day I will complete my work/goal'" (13:32).

In addition to performing his healing activity, Jesus continues to speak of its significance in his mission.

A second, related point in this important text is the way in which Jesus informs the reader that healing is a not insignificant aspect of his gospel proclamation, but rather is itself gospel proclamation. As the gospel according to Luke unfolds, it becomes clear that the relationship between word and deed leaves neither word nor deed in a position of primacy: both bear testimony to the inbreaking kingdom of God.

It is also significant that Jesus' healing activity is tied to his anointing by the Spirit. It is clear that he takes the action he does in the synagogue in Luke 4 owing to the fact that he is full of the Holy Spirit, as a result of the Spirit's anointing at his baptism. Apparently, the anointing by the Spirit empowers his healing ministry throughout the gospel, and this is at times made explicit by reference to healing power present in and/or leaving his body. For example, Luke 5:17 notes that the power of the Lord was present to heal the sick. Similarly, in a text devoted to his ministry to crowds that came from Judea and Jerusalem, and as far away as Tyre and Sidon, one reads:

> "These came to hear him and to be healed from their diseases; and those troubled by unclean spirits were being healed. And the whole crowd was seeking to touch him, because power was coming out from him and healing all" (6:18-19).

Significantly, this text is the preamble to the "Sermon on the Plain" in Luke (6:17-49), which is devoted to Jesus' teaching in word. This theme is developed later in the gospel when Jesus himself says, in response to the woman with an issue of blood who "touches" him, "Who touched me? For I know that power has gone out from me" (8:46).

Still another important aspect of the Luke 4 text is the intimate connection between physical healing and salvation in the ministry of Jesus. While there may be a sense in which all the healing activity that follows conveys salvation to the recipients; this connection is made explicit at several points in the following narrative. At the conclusion of the story of the healing of the woman with the issue of blood, Jesus says, "Daughter, your faith has saved you; go in peace" (8:48). Later in the gospel, one finds the story of the ten lepers whom Jesus makes clean (17:11-19). After they have been cleansed (v. 14), one of them finds that he has been healed, returns glorifying God with a loud voice, falls at the feet of Jesus and thanks him. To this cleansed and healed Samaritan Jesus says, "Rising, go; your faith has saved you" (v. 19). Finally, in the Lukan version of the healing of the blind man (18:35-43), the text reads:

> "And Jesus said to him, 'Receive your sight; your faith has saved you. And at once he received his sight and followed him, glorifying God" (vs. 42-43a).

The role of the Twelve as participants in Jesus' healing and preaching ministry is even more explicit in Luke than in Matthew and Mark. For the story devoted to their call, commission and sending (Luke 9:1-6) contains three separate references to their healing activity, as a reading of the text makes clear:

> "And calling the Twelve together he gave them power and authority over all demons and to heal diseases, and he sent them to preach the

kingdom of God and to heal" (vv.1-2). "…And going out they went from village to village preaching the good news and healing everywhere" (v. 6).

Returning, the apostles reported to Jesus everything they had done (v. 10). However, participation in the healing ministry of Jesus is not limited to the Twelve according to Luke, for one chapter later (10:1-24) Jesus sends out the Seventy[-Two], instructing them to heal the sick and to preach that the kingdom of God is near (v. 9). Upon their return, they report that even the demons were subject to them in Jesus' name (v. 17). By this means, the reader of these Lukan texts is prepared for the activity of the disciples in the narrative of the Acts of the Apostles, Luke's continuation of the gospel's story.

A final note about the relationship between miracles of healing and mission is related to the response that these miracles generate in the gospel according to Luke. Often a miracle of healing leads to amazement, faith or praise of God on the part of the one who is healed or on the parts of those who witness the healing (5:25-26; 7:16, 17; 9:43; 13:17; 18:43). This emphasis is also a dominant one in Luke's second volume.

The following questions are designed to facilitate reflection and discussion.

1) What is the relationship between the Spirit and healing in the gospel according to Luke?

2) Are there people you know or communities with which you are familiar that are characterized by the Spirit's anointing to heal the sick and cast out demons?

3) In what ways has the Spirit empowered you to "heal" those who suffer?

John 4:5-30   Nina Lundgren

So he came to a Samaritan city called Sychar, near the plot of
ground that Jacob had given to his son Joseph. Jacob's well was there,
and Jesus, tired out by his journey, was sitting by the well. It was
about noon. A Samaritan woman came to draw water, and Jesus
said to her, "Give me a drink." (His disciples had gone to the city to
buy food.) The Samaritan woman said to him, "How is it that you,
a Jew, ask a drink of me, a woman of Samaria?" (Jews do not share
things in common with Samaritans.) Jesus answered her, "If you
knew the gift of God, and who it is that is saying to you, "Give me a
drink,' you would have asked him, and he would have given you
living water." The woman said to him, "Sir, you have no bucket, and
the well is deep. Where do you get that living water? Are you
greater than our ancestor Jacob, who gave us the well, and with his
sons and his flocks drank from it?" Jesus said to her, "Everyone who
drinks of this water will be thirsty again, but those who drink of the
water that I will give them will never be thirsty. The water that I
will give will become in them a spring of water gushing up to eternal life." The woman said to him, "Sir, give me this water, so that I
may never be thirsty or have to keep coming here to draw water."
Jesus said to her, "Go, call your husband, and come back." The
woman answered him, "I have no husband." Jesus said to her, "You
are right in saying, "I have no husband'; for you have had five husbands, and the one you have now is not your husband. What you
have said is true!" The woman said to him, "Sir, I see that you are
a prophet. Our ancestors worshiped on this mountain, but you say
that the place where people must worship is in Jerusalem." Jesus
said to her, "Woman, believe me, the hour is coming when you will
worship the Father neither on this mountain nor in Jerusalem. You

> *worship what you do not know; we worship what we know, for salvation is from the Jews. But the hour is coming, and is now here, when the true worshipers will worship the Father in spirit and truth, for the Father seeks such as these to worship him. God is spirit, and those who worship him must worship in spirit and truth." The woman said to him, "I know that Messiah is coming" (who is called Christ). "When he comes, he will proclaim all things to us." Jesus said to her, "I am he, the one who is speaking to you." Just then his disciples came. They were astonished that he was speaking with a woman, but no one said, "What do you want?" or, "Why are you speaking with her?" Then the woman left her water jar and went back to the city. She said to the people, "Come and see a man who told me everything I have ever done! He cannot be the Messiah, can he?" They left the city and were on their way to him.*

Let me tell you about a woman who lived in a town called Sychar in the region of Samaria. She and the other people who lived there were called "Samaritans". She had experienced many difficulties in her life, and she knew that sometimes she had behaved badly. She did not always feel good about herself.

One day she went to fetch water from the well. It was the middle of the day, and Jesus was passing through Sychar. He had settled down to rest by the well. It was called "Jacob's well", and it was one of the most important places in the town because everyone depended on it for water. When the woman came to the well, she could see that Jesus was a Jew. The Jews and Samaritans were suspicious of each other, so the woman tried to avoid Jesus at first. She was surprised when he spoke to her, asking if she would help him get water from the well. He was thirsty from walking in the heat of the day.

The woman was still reluctant to talk with Jesus, since she was Samaritan and he was Jewish, but he began to speak of the "living water" that God provides for all people. The woman became confused, and asked him how he could offer water when he didn't have a dipper or a bucket or a pitcher to use at the well. Jesus described another source of living water, a bubbling stream that brought people the refreshing water of eternal life. The woman realized this was something she needed, and she asked Jesus where she could find such water so that she would never be thirsty again.

Jesus asked about her husband, and the woman had to admit that the man with whom she lived was not her husband, although she had been married five times. She may have been afraid that

Jesus would reject her because of the way she lived, or possibly he would ignore her or fail to take her seriously. But just then a strange thing happened. Jesus began to describe her life, and things she had done, and even though he was a stranger to her, everything he said was true. She realized that Jesus was a prophet, and she asked him questions about things that were important to her. Jesus told her everything she wanted – and needed – to know. He also encouraged her to worship God, the creator of all people.

Jesus took her seriously, and that was important to her. He listened to what she had to say, and he told her the truth. At the end of their conversation, Jesus told her that he was the promised Messiah, sent by God, the helper and liberator of all people. The woman left her things by the well, rushing back through town to tell her neighbours of the amazing man she had met at Jacob's well.

After that meeting, Jesus stayed in Samaria for a time and then continued to travel the countryside with his disciples – who had been as surprised as anyone that he had talked with a Samaritan woman, and that she had been so full of joy when they saw her hurry away, and that her friends came to appreciate Jesus, too. For the woman, life had changed dramatically. She had regained respect for herself. She realized that she was someone who could be taken seriously, even by Jesus. She realized that God's salvation was intended for everyone – not just for a certain sort of person, or a particular race or nation.

Things to discuss

- How do you think this woman felt when Jesus first spoke to her?
- Why do you think she felt that way?
- Have you ever been surprised that someone bothered to speak to you? If so, how did you feel?
- What has someone said to you that made you very happy?
- Have you ever said anything to someone else that made that person happy?
- How can a conversation give someone encouragement? Can you give an example?
- Why do you think Jesus talked about "living water"? What did he mean?

Things to do with children

- If possible, build a "well" using a large container of water. Let the children use dippers, cups, pitchers and glasses to offer water to one another. Remember to have towels on hand.

- Let children act out the story, with discussion afterwards. Characters might represent the woman, Jesus, the disciples (Jews), the townspeople (Samaritans).

- Let them draw pictures depicting the "living water" that quenches thirst and gives life.

- Help them to give one another positive feedback, telling one another what they admire about each person present, offering encouragement, showing respect. Ask if there are people they know who need to hear positive things about themselves.

- The greatest resource you have as a leader is yourself. Use your imagination, your own reflections, experiences and feelings.

2 Called in Christ to Be Reconciling and Healing Communities

Romans 12:1-21   Peter A. Chamberas

I appeal to you therefore, brothers and sisters, by the mercies of God, to present your bodies as a living sacrifice, holy and acceptable to God, which is your spiritual worship. Do not be conformed to this world, but be transformed by the renewing of your minds, so that you may discern what is the will of god – what is good and acceptable and perfect. For by the grace given to me I say to everyone among you not to think of yourself more highly than you ought to think, but to think with sober judgement, each according to the measure of faith that God has assigned. For as in one body we have many members, and not all the members have the same function, so we, who are many, are one body in Christ, and individually we are members one of another. We have gifts that differ according to the grace given to us: prophecy, in proportion to faith; ministry, in ministering; the teacher, in teaching; the exhorter, in exhortation; the giver, in generosity; the leader, in diligence; the compassionate, in cheerfulness. Let love be genuine; hate what is evil, hold fast to what is good; love one another with mutual affection; outdo one another in showing honor. Do not lag in zeal, be ardent in spirit, serve the Lord. Rejoice in hope, be patient in suffering, persevere in prayer. Contribute to the needs of the saints; extend hospitality to strangers. Bless those who persecute you; bless and do not curse them. Rejoice with those who rejoice, weep with those who weep. Live in harmony with one another; do not be haughty, but associate with the lowly, do not claim to be wiser than you are. Do not repay anyone evil for evil, but take thought for what is noble, in the sight of all. If it is possible, so far as it depends on you, live peaceably with all. Beloved, never avenge yourselves, but leave it to the wrath of God; for it is written, *"Vengeance is mine, I will repay, says the Lord." No, "if your enemies are hungry, feed them; if they are thirsty, give them something to drink; for by doing this you will heap burning coals on their heads." Do not be overcome by evil, but overcome evil with good.*

Orthodox Christian life is by no means characterized only by doctrines and beliefs that are of a theoretical nature. Christianity is a way of life imbued by the Word of God in the sacred scripture of the church. Orthodoxia (right or true belief) must be complemented by *orthopraxia* (right or true action or way of life). As Christians, we cannot live as we wish nor do those things which are often prompted by our fallen nature. We are challenged to transcend our human inclinations that draw us into conformity with this world, and to be transformed by the renewal of our mind and way of life according to the stature of our Lord Jesus Christ.

Commentary and interpretation

In his great letter to the Romans, St. Paul, having concluded his rather systematic theological argument in chapters 1-11, turns typically, in chapter 12, to the moral and ethical consequences of Christian doctrine for practical living in the Christian community. Christian faith is inseparable from Christian conduct. In trying to understand the relationship between faith and life, doctrine and ethics, it is important to avoid a common misunderstanding by arranging these two elements too neatly under the notions of "theory" and "practice", as if there is a system of maxims and directions for Christian living as distinct from Christian theology. In fact, St. Paul wants us to understand that every action of the believer is based upon the previous action of God in Christ: It is precisely because of what God has done in Christ that Christians are called to respond in a faith that works itself out in live and service. This means that St. Paul's exhortations for Christian living are really another way of expressing the gospel of salvation in Jesus Christ.

When St. Paul, in Romans 12:1, begins his appeal to the Roman Christians "by the mercies of God", he is in effect reminding them of the entire previous doctrinal part of his letter. His saying that all subsequent counsel about conduct springs from the previous declaration of doctrine. The new relationship between God and humanity, established by the love of God in Christ, awakens in the faithful an appropriate response, obliging them to be consecrated to God's service.

The vitality of a Christian is seen in a new life that is offered to God, and dedicate to serving the will of God in all we are and do. The truest sacrifice is to live according to God's will, and the truest freedom is found in the most dedicate service and worship of God. The Christian gospel requires that lives must be cleansed by repentance and renewal; they must be marked by holiness that is expressed by discipline of ordinary experiences in daily life. To worship God in truth and spirit is to dedicate ourselves to him without reserve, so that the moral quality of our life may correspond consistently with the will of God.

The prevailing weakness in the Christianity of our day is increasing acceptance of the dominant intellectual, moral and social atmosphere of the age. We too readily conform to the outward fashions and conventions which our society dictates. When our alertness to evil is disarmed, we drift into agreement with the ever changing things the world demands. Therefore, St. Paul reminds Christians of every age: "Do not be conformed to this world, but be transformed by renewal of your mind, that you may prove what is the will of God". The new age which God has inaugurated in Christ requires a new and risen life in the Christian community. This newness is not a matter of chronological time, but a newness of character and nature. The children of the world have been made the children of God, and they must live accordingly. When Christ comes into a man's life he is a new man; when Christ comes into a woman's life she is a new woman; his/her mind is different, transforming essentially because the mind of Christ is in him/her. It is the very decisive power of God's Spirit, with God's transforming effect upon our lives, that makes it possible for us to discern and to prove "what is the will of God". Thus we discover in our actual situation what God would have us do, as we find our place and discharge our responsibilities in the reconciling and healing Christian community.

While it is a personal obligation of every Christian to discover and experience the possibilities of the new life in Christ, it is certainly not an individual achievement. "*Unus Christianus — nullus Christianus*" (One Christian is no Christian). Nobody could be a Christian alone, as an isolated individual, but only together with the other brothers and sisters in Christ. From the very beginning Christianity existed as a corporate reality; to be a Christian meant that one belonged to the church. But it was not a community based on social cohesion, mutual affection, or any other natural attraction. Christian existence presumes an incorporation, a membership in the apostolic community, which was gathered and constituted by Jesus himself. Christians are united not only among themselves, but first of all they are one in Christ. This prior communion with Christ makes the communion of all the brothers and sisters first possible in him.

A favorite thought of St. Paul is of the church as a body (cf. 1 Cor. 12:12-27). The members of the body neither argue with each other, nor envy each other, nor dispute about their relative importance. Each part of the body carries out its own function, however humble that function may be. The Christian community, Paul believed, should be like that. Each member has a task to do; and it is only when each contributes the help of his own task that the body of community functions as it should.

Any inflated notion of our importance distorts our self-awareness and jeopardizes our proper relationship with others. Christian fellowship requires modesty, sober judgement and true insight, which spring from real. Christian humility, which in turn comes to us with the standard of faith given to us as a gift of grace from God. An honest assessment of our own capabilities, without conceit and without false modesty, is one of the first essentials of a useful life. We are to use the gift God has given us, as best as we can, even if it is a humble one. We are not to envy some one else's gift, and regret that some other gift has not been to us. Every *charisma* comes from God and must be used, not for our own prestige, but with the conviction that it is our duty and privilege to make our contribution, however humble, for the common good of the whole community and of the individual members. A sense of interdependence with others and the proper understanding and discharge of our responsibilities within the Christian community will not only teach us to use the aptitudes committed to us by God for welfare of the whole body, but it will also lift us up to a closer and more authentic relationship with Christ.

While St. Paul had no sympathy with spectacular exhibits of religious gifts that do not edify the faithful, he was quick to emphasize that gifts be used to achieve the purpose for which it is intended. Even the very practical gifts of helpfulness must be practiced in the appropriate spirit of kindness and cheerfulness, and never be degenerated into lifeless and disagreeable duties.

In verses 9-13, St. Paul lists many practical rules for ordinary, everyday Christian living. First in this list is the virtue of true and authentic love, which is always the ultimate goal of our Christian life, both within the church and outside of it. St. Paul has much to say about the appropriate response of all believers. "We love because he first loved us" (1 John 4:19). This love must be extended not only to God (verses 1-2) and to other believers (verses 3-13, 15-16), but also to those outside the church and particularly to enemies, wherever they may be (verses 14.17-21). Here again, these timeless exhortations to practice a variety of virtues remind us that true Christian faith must work itself out in genuine and profound love. Christian love must be absolutely sincere; pretense and hypocrisy can never co-exist with genuine and authentic love. Love also must not be relegated to a superficial sentimentalism that is devoid of any moral and spiritual reality that clearly discerns and discriminates between the basic forces of good an evil.

The presence of true love has many practical results: we respect others and treat them with brotherly affection; we avoid false estimates of ourselves and given proper and prompt recognition and honor to the worth of others, we acquire not only the ability to sympathize with those who suffer but also to rejoice in the success of others; we contribute to the needs of others and provide gracious hospitality, we live in harmony with others. A Christian will give himself to any task, however humble, with zeal and earnest commitment, knowing that it is motivated by the Spirit of God, who sets us aglow, and that through such tasks he or she can truly and effectively serve the Lord.

What God has done for us illuminates what God will do for us in the future. Christians are persuaded that God loves them, that Jesus Christ has made possible a more abundant and richer life for them in his church. This kind of hope leads to joy, because where there is spiritual growth and true life in God, there is also radiance and joy. Because St. Paul knew that adversity is not absent from life and that it often provides spiritual good and growth, he exhorts all Christians to be patient in their tribulations and constant in their life of prayer. Christian faith is not a guarantee of deliverance from misfortune; it is the promise that in the midst of tribulation and suffering we shall be sustained and strengthened. Half-hearted and slothful attitudes in practicing the presence of God, particularly in prayer and worship, will never suffice to create and maintain a Christian life. Throughout his letters, St. Paul places great emphasis on the demand for sustained and strenuous effort in our Christian life.

In the final verses (14, 17-21) of chapter 12, St. Paul turns his attention to another series of rules and principles to govern our relationship with our fellow human beings, who may be outside of the church or who may be our enemies. Rather than curse, we are to bless, to speak well of and pray for those who persecute us. In this stark contrast we are prompted by the love of Christ. What are we to do if we suffer evil? At last we are not to repay the transgressor in kind, evil for evil. Christian love requires that is transcend evil and manifest itself in the good that transforms (cf. Mt. 5:46-47; 1 Cor. 13:5-7). On the question of vengeance (v. 19), St. Paul raises the problem to the level of God's relationship with all of us. If we resort to reprisals we are encroaching on the prerogatives of God; we are seizing powers which do not belong to us. We must leave this matter to the righteous judgement of God. The ultimate overthrow of evil is in God's hands. We must therefore resist the temptation to retaliate by reflecting on the high truths of Christian doctrine regarding God's righteous and beneficent purpose in a universe where moral and spiritual as well as physical and material laws pursue their appointed course.

In authentic Christian living, it is not enough simply to refrain from judgement and retaliation; we must also be prepared to offer active aid to our enemy where his need is most acute. If he is hungry, we must feed him; if he is thirsty, we must give him drink. This is the Christian law of love which allows the sinner to see himself with hope and mercy, without an emotional need to defend himself. Through this act of love an enemy is confronted with the holy will of God, who, in such circumstances, is like "a consuming fire" for the purpose of cleaning and purity.

In the final exhortation of this passage: "Do not be overcome by evil, but overcome evil with good", St. Paul wants to express the overarching Christian truth that victory remains with love. Goodness can be overcome by evil, if evil is allowed to take control and dictate to us the terms on which human relations will be conducted. The element of hope in our entangled and difficult human situations is goodness of Christian living. As children of God, we do not rely on our clever skills but on spiritual powers which we can apprehend and appropriate through our belief that God co-operated for good with those who love him. This closing counsel of St. Paul sums up everything he has been saying about our relationship with those who are opposed to us. It is epitome of the characteristic attitude of the entire New Testament to all problems of human conduct. This attitude expresses so faithfully all that is most distinctive in the life and teaching of Jesus Christ, who is the inspiration of all the thought and conduct of St. Paul. In the final analysis, the essence of Christian discipleship is a personal commitment to God's will in Jesus Christ.

When believers function authentically as described by St. Paul in Romans 12, we can indeed have reconciled and healed Christians, who hopefully will be able to create reconciling and healing communities. This can indeed happen not only because "God was in Christ reconciling the world to himself" (2 Co. 5:19), but also because we in turn have reconciled ourselves to God. Not only in Christ in our midst, but we too are manifestly in Christ through the power of the Holy Spirit. While this is a present reality here and now, it is also our constant, fervent hope and prayer for the future: come, Holy Spirit, heal and reconcile! We want to be transfigured into that wonderful way of life, which truly transforms us into healing and reconciling communities.

Suggestions and questions for further reflection:

1. Each member of the study group should read and study the biblical passage in advance by becoming familiar with its general context in the Bible. Other familiar and related passages may be sought out for comparison.

2. The study group may approach the text in a meditative and prayerful attitude by starting with a prayer for guidance and enlightenment to understand and to appreciate the Word of God.

3. Each person may attempt to read the passage as a message from God directed personally to each of us, requiring a personal response of obedience.

4. Is a personal response of obedience possible to the exhortations of our passage? Which exhortations do you think are easier to apply to our life, and which are more difficult and why?

5. If we accept the Bible as the authoritative Word of God in human language, as having both, a divine and a human nature, what elements in our passage may be considered to be divine element and which the human? ➤

6. In Orthodox Christianity, the church and the Bible are interdependent and inseparable. In what ways, if any, do you think the passage under discussion bears this truth out?

7. If, as many Christians believe today, Christianity has reached an impasse because Christians have failed to be truly Christian, how does our passage shed light on our predicament? How does it point to the formation of a new humanity? How can it help us create healing and reconciling communities?

1 Samuel 3:1-21 M. Campbell

N*ow the boy Samuel was ministering to the Lord under Eli. The word of the Lord was rare in those days; visions were not widespread. At that time Eli, whose eyesight had begun to grow dim so that he could not see, was lying down in his room; the lamp of God had not yet gone out, and Samuel was lying down in the temple of the Lord, where the ark of God was. Then the Lord called, "Samuel! Samuel!" and he said, "Here I am!" and ran to Eli, and said, "Here I am, for you called me." But he said, "I did not call; lie down again." So he went and lay down. The Lord called again, "Samuel!" Samuel got up and went to Eli, and said, "Here I am, for you called me." But he said, "I did not call, my son; lie down again." Now Samuel did not yet know the Lord, and the word of the Lord had not yet been revealed to him. The Lord called Samuel again, a third time. And he got up and went to Eli, and said, "Here I am, for you called me." Then Eli perceived that the Lord was calling the boy. Therefore Eli said to Samuel, "Go, lie down; and if he calls you, you shall say, "Speak, Lord, for your servant is listening.' " So Samuel went and lay down in his place. Now the Lord came and stood there, calling as before, "Samuel! Samuel!" And Samuel said, "Speak, for your servant is listening." Then the Lord said to Samuel, "See, I am about to do something in Israel that will make both ears of anyone who hears of it tingle. On that day I will fulfill against Eli all that I have spoken concerning his house, from beginning to end. For I have told him that I am about to punish his house forever, for the iniquity that he knew, because his sons were blaspheming God, and he did not restrain them. Therefore I swear to the house of Eli that the iniquity of Eli's house shall not be expiated by sacrifice or offering forever." Samuel lay there until morning; then he opened the doors of the house of the Lord. Samuel was afraid to tell the vision*

> to Eli. But Eli called Samuel and said, "Samuel, my son." He said, "Here I am." Eli said, "What was it that he told you? Do not hide it from me. May God do so to you and more also, if you hide anything from me of all that he told you." So Samuel told him everything and hid nothing from him. Then he said, "It is the Lord; let him do what seems good to him." As Samuel grew up, the Lord was with him and let none of his words fall to the ground. And all Israel from Dan to Beer-sheba knew that Samuel was a trustworthy

This study will affirm the significance of celebrating our identity in community. It will also highlight the Call of Samuel as a context for exploring the roles God may be giving us and calling us to play within God's global community.

Introductory activity

Preparation and Supplies

- A ball of yarn or string
- Large piece of paper or poster board
- Markers

Leader's Notes

Gather the children into a circle. Invite them to define the word "community". (It might simply be described as a gathering or group of people.) Name the municipality where most of your participants live and ask them how long they think it has been in existence. Identify some of the families represented in your circle and invite them to guess how many generations have gone before them? Point out that the roles and relationships people have with each other usually define or determine the length of time they stay together. Introduce "Community Connections" activity to visualize how various roles and relationships characterize the dynamics of community within a family or a municipality. Demonstrate the game in the following way.

Throw a ball of yarn or string to someone in your circle and ask him/her to name a role that a family member might play, e.g. mother, father, sister, brother, son, daughter, grandparent, aunt, uncle or cousin. Then, invite your first participant to hold onto the end piece of yarn or string and throw the ball to others in the circle, encouraging him or her to do the same. Stop periodically, to view the web that your circle is weaving as you expand the options to include roles people play in relation to each other in your municipality, e.g. teacher, student, pastor, church people, friend and a variety of community services workers, such as police officers, firefighters, postal workers, doctors, nurses, lawyers, auto mechanics, etc.

As you conclude this activity, recognize that communities are shaped by the many roles, relationships and connections people make with each other. Point out that God gives everyone special interests and abilities to play specific roles towards each other.

Introduce the Bible story for this day. Identify Samuel as a boy in the Bible who was invited to play a role for the People of Israel in Old Testament times.

Story Presentation

Read or act out the following story:

There was a boy named Samuel who lived in the temple with an older priest named Eli. He was a good boy and God was pleased with him. In fact, God decided there was a special job for him to do. One night, while Samuel was sleeping, God called out to Samuel in a voice that he could hear. Samuel had never heard God speak to him before and so he thought it must be Eli. Samuel went to Eli and said, "Here am I, for you have called me." Eli was surprised to see him, because he hadn't called for him. "Go back and lie down. Samuel. I didn't call for you." God called out his name two more times and each time Samuel went to Eli, thinking it must be him. Finally Eli told him that it must be God calling out to his name. He told Samuel that if he heard his name again, he should acknowledge it as a call from God. Eli advised him to say, "Speak, Lord, for your servant is listening." Samuel went back to bed and, once again, God called out to him. This time, Samuel said, "Speak, Lord, for your servant is listening" and God proceeded to give him a special message. The next morning, Samuel told Eli what God had told him and Eli recognized Samuel as a messenger of Gods Word. Samuel devoted his time, gifts and abilities to serving God and others through the job God had called him to do. (An adaptation of 1 Samuel 1-3)

Interpreting the Story: Special Invitations!

Make or purchase an invitation with the words, "You're invited" on the front of the card. Display the card and invite children to describe some of the invitations they receive. Mention that we might also receive invitations on the phone or in person. Clarify that not all invitations are for parties or celebrations. Point out that people are often invited to share their time, talents and abilities in leadership and service to a specific group or community in need.

Discussion Questions:

1) How did God send an invitation to Samuel? [Answer : A dream or a voice in the night] What did God want him to do or be? [Answer: To hear God's voice and be a messenger of God's Word to God's people.]

2) What role did Eli play in encouraging Samuel to do God's will? [He acknowledged that his call was from God.] Who encourages you to use your God-given gifts and abilities to serve God and others?

Gifted-wrapped for Community

Preparation and Supplies
- Copies of the "Mini-Me" gift, hands & feet pattern sheet
- Scissors
- Tape or glue
- Markers
- Two coloured strips of paper (In the US, two 8 _ inch by 1 inch strips, and two 11 inch by 1 inch strips; in areas where A-4 sized paper is standard, two 21 cm by 3 cm and two 30 cm by 3 cm strips)

Leader's Notes

Make a sample of a gift-wrapped "mini-me". Cut out the gift, gift tag, hands and feet. Decorate the gift, colouring the eyes, hair and shoes to match yours. Fold the strips, accordion-style, into one-half to one-inch segments. Attach one end of the shorter strips to either side of the gift and the other end to the hand pieces. Then, attach one end of the longer strips to the bottom of the gift and the other end to the shoe pieces. Print some of your own interests, talents and abilities on the gift tag, e.g. music, reading, praying for others, and attach it to the top of the gift. Display your gift-wrapped "mini-me" as you identify it as a mini-version of you. Explain that we have all been gift-wrapped with talents and abilities to serve God and others in the communities in which we reside, e.g. our families, God's family or church and local municipalities. God invites us to be God's hands and feet and voice to speak as we make the most of the talents and abilities that God has given us. We need to be ready and willing as God urges us from within our hearts or prompts others to invite us. Just like Samuel, we must be good listeners and willing servants.

Invite the children to make a gift-wrapped "mini-me". Encourage them to name some interests, talents and abilities they've been given to share.

At Your Service!

Remind your participants that every person has been gift-wrapped with special talents and abilities to be God's "hands and feet or voice to speak". God calls us to serve God and others by using our God given talents and abilities to play special roles for each other. When we are invited to use our talents and abilities, we should consider it an invitation from God and respond willingly.

Initiate a brief dialogue with each one of your participants. Call out each name and invite each one to respond by repeating their name and asking them to respond, "I'm at your service, Lord !", and encourage them to identify one talent, interest or ability they printed on their gift tag.

Close your time together with prayer, thanking God for the many communities in which you live and for the many ways God calls or invites us to share our God-given gifts in service to others.

3 *Healing in a World of Exclusion and Violence*

John 4:1-26, 39-42, Genesis 37-45
L.J. Andersson

John 4:1-26 and 39-42

*N*ow when Jesus learned that the Pharisees had heard, "Jesus is making and baptizing more disciples than John" – although it was not Jesus himself but his disciples who baptized – he left Judea and started back to Galilee. But he had to go through Samaria. So he came to a Samaritan city called Sychar, near the plot of ground that Jacob had given to his son Joseph. Jacob's well was there, and Jesus, tired out by his journey, was sitting by the well. It was about noon. A Samaritan woman came to draw water, and Jesus said to her, "Give me a drink". (His disciples had gone to the city to buy food). The Samaritan woman said to him, "How is it that you, a Jew, ask a drink of me, a woman of Samaria?" (Jews do not share things in common with Samaritans). Jesus answered her, "If you knew the gift of God, and who it is that is saying to you, 'Give me a drink,' you would have asked him, and he would have given you living water." The woman said to him, "Sir, you have no bucket, and the well is deep. Where do you get that living water? Are you greater than our ancestor Jacob, who gave us the well, and with his sons and his flocks drank from it?" Jesus said to her, "Everyone who drinks of this water will be thirsty again, but those who drink of the water that I will give them will never be thirsty. The water that I will give will become in them a spring of water gushing up to eternal life." The woman said to him, "Sir, give me this water, so that I may never be thirsty or have to keep coming here to draw water." Jesus said to her, "Go, call your husband, and come back." The woman answered him, "I have no husband." Jesus said to her, "You are right in saying, 'I have no husband'; for you have had five husbands, and the one you have now is not your husband. What you have said is *true!" The woman said to him, "Sir, I see that you are a prophet. Our ancestors worshipped on this mountain, but you say that the place where people must worship is in Jerusalem." Jesus said to her, "Woman, believe me, the hour is coming when you will worship the Father neither on this mountain nor in Jerusalem. You worship what you do not know; we worship what we know, for salvation is from the Jews. But the hour is coming, and is now here, when the true worshippers will worship the Father in spirit and truth, for the Father seeks such as these to worship him. God is spirit, and those who worship him must worship in spirit and truth." The woman said to him, "I know that Messiah is coming" (who is called Christ). "When he comes, he will proclaim all things to us." Jesus said to her, "I am he, the one who is speaking to you." (...) Many Samaritans from that city believed in him because of the woman's testimony, "He told me everything I have ever done." So when the Samaritans came to him, they asked him to stay with them; and he stayed there two days. And many more believed because of his word. They said to the woman, "It is no longer because of what you said that we believe, for we have heard for ourselves, and we know that this is truly the Saviour of the world".*

I recently read a novel by one of the most famous authors in Sweden. The story is about a woman who moves to a little village in the north of Sweden. She comes there to work as a Lutheran pastor and to search for her roots. The woman has not grown up with her parents. As a baby she was adopted by another family. She knows that her mother is dead, but she wants to find her father, whom she has never seen. Finally they meet and her father is filled with guilt because he neglected his child. She is a Christian, but he is not. There is one thing she wants to say, but the words won´t come from her mouth. What she wants to say is this: I live in a world where forgiveness exists! That is her way to summarize the Christian faith. It is not a bad way!

The story about Jesus and his meeting with the woman at the well is a story about forgiveness. I do not think that this woman belongs to the lower class of society. She does not throw herself at the feet of Jesus; in fact, she is a bit harsh in speaking with him and she does not seem insecure. Perhaps she is someone of social substance. Maybe her life with many different men is a well-hidden secret – except to Him who knows the darkness we carry inside.

In John 1:14 it is said that Jesus is filled with truth and grace. He gives the gifts of truth and grace to the woman in a perfect balance. If he had started to accuse the woman for her sinful life, their talk probably would have ended there. No, he places a measure of grace in one side of the scales, before he puts a grain of painful truth in the other. In that moment the woman appears ready to receive the bitter cup as well as the one that quenches her thirst. Why? She has been understood. Her lust for men is not abnormal, but she has underestimated her own deep thirst for a life worth living. Jesus has reminded her of that thirst, and with the living water in sight the woman can drink the bitter cup as well. She admits to herself: I am a sinner. The offering Jesus gives of living water isn't cheap, it will cost the son of God his life on Calvary. It is not cheap, but it is free. The grace of God has a high price, but that price is not paid by us. We could never afford it.

The change that occurs in this woman is evident. Afterwards, she walks right into the town of Sychar, and she is eager for the people there to find what she has found. The fact that she went to the well at the hour of the day when no one else was there may indicate that she was excluded from the fellowship of the other women. So perhaps there had been rumours about the woman and all her men. Her willingness to share the good news with the people in town indicates that she has forgiven them for isolating her. That is a vital aspect of forgiveness, to give to others what we have received; otherwise we, as is said in the New Testament, "insult the spirit of grace". Even more, the woman has forgiven herself. I think that is shown in her boldness. She walks boldly into Sychar, thrusting herself forward as an evangelist. She finds herself worthy of this important task.

Is there a fourth aspect of forgiveness? It may sound odd, but some of us some time in our lives feel the need to forgive God. We live in a world of exclusion and violence. Some of us are seriously damaged by the evil of this world. If we believe in an Almighty and a good God, questions will arise. Where were you, God, when I suffered? Didn´t you see my pain? Do you really care? How can we understand all this? A parable in Matthew 13 has been helpful to me. Jesus tells the story about a man who sows good seed in his field. The next night an enemy is there and sows weeds among the good seed. The owner of the field explains that he can´t pick up the weeds right away. There is a risk that he would harm or uproot the good seed. The two plants have to grow together until the day of harvest, when the good seed is finally to be separated from the weeds. We can in no way deny that good seed has been planted in this world: there is so much beauty, goodness and mercy. Evidence of the devil's works are also clear. We are called to live amid this mixture. No one of us can avoid all pain. As children, with a childlike attitude towards God our Father it is natural and perhaps necessary to cry: "Where are you God, are we forgotten?" In that process of pain and healing, we can speak in terms of "forgiving God".

In his talk with the woman at the well, Jesus opens a window to this aspect of reconciliation. This happens when he states that the Father seeks worshippers who will worship in spirit and in truth. Another way to express this is that the Father desires that the prayer of our hearts should be the prayer of our lips. The Lord doesn´t want us to hide from God's presence in any situation.

One good way to learn something about true worship is to read or pray the psalms. There, nothing is hidden or forbidden in the dialogue between God and humankind. Praise and mourning, faith and doubt are mixed and of equal worth before God, when offered up as genuine prayer from the depths of our being.

I think that a key concept in the practice of forgiveness is to understand and to be understood.

As I write this, a young girl is in my thoughts. She is hurt inside, and the sad thing is that it is her mother who caused this pain. Will the girl ever be able to forgive? Maybe, when she gets help to understand that her mother is not fully sane, but suffering from a psychological illness. This young girl has developed a behaviour that is not always easy to cope with. Will people in her surroundings forgive her for her seemingly inappropriate behaviour? Yes, I believe they will, when they understand the difficult circumstances under which this girl has been living. Will she forgive herself? Yes, if she gets enough love and support from caring people who do not shut their eyes for her needs. Finally, as a small child this girl put her trust in God, and sadly that trust is now damaged. Can it be healed? That is my hope and my intercession.

A dear friend of mine who has been through a lot of suffering once said: It is astonishing how much we can survive if we find some place where we can cry, and if we find someone who is genuinely willing to listen to our story. Some of us find all this in God. Many of us need to see God's image in the human face of one who says, "I am willing to share your burden."

Genesis 37-45

In Genesis chapter 37-45 we can learn more about forgiveness. There we find one of the most beautiful stories in the Old Testament. Joseph, the beloved son of Jacob and Rachel, becomes his older brothers' enemy. They envy him his special gifts and the fact that he is so obviously the favourite son of his parents. The brothers' feelings are not hard to understand. We all need the love of our parents, and we fear being rejected. We can understand, but not defend, what the brothers do in their envy. They sell Joseph as a slave and bring the false news to Jacob that Joseph is dead. After many years the brothers meet Joseph again. By this time, Joseph is an honoured official in Egypt. It becomes clear that the loss of his family was in no way compensated by the imperial power and glory he exercises in Egypt. That part of the story is a beautiful symbol of what really counts in our lives. The story ends in a very moving scene of forgiveness, healing and restored relations between Joseph and his brothers.

Before this takes place, Joseph in a very subtle way reminds his brothers of their guilt. They see it clearly, the regret it deeply, and they confess their sin. That is how we know the tears, the hugs and the talk between the brothers are genuine. True reconciliation cannot take place without awareness of guilt and repentance.

Another beautiful detail in the story about Joseph is that he gets to see his father again. He is with him when he dies. Perhaps that was Joseph´s prayer during the years of separation. When it comes to the loss of loved ones in life, it is not possible to recover everything one has lost. Still, there are often "small" gains to be found, that can bring so much comfort and hope. He who has said of himself that he came to seek and restore the lost, will help us to find this comfort (Luke 19:10).

Whatever is not restored, we can survive, so long as we find a place to cry and someone who will listen to our story.

Questions

John 4

1. Think about these four aspects of forgiveness:
a. What can help us to receive forgiveness?
b. What can help us to forgive those who have hurt us?
c. Why is it sometimes hard to forgive ourselves? What can help us?
d. How can we help a friend who feels that it is God who should ask for forgiveness, or that the Almighty hasn´t done the job properly?

Genesis 37-50

2. What can we learn about exclusion and forgiveness from the story about Joseph and his brothers? Somewhere in this story, do we recognize ourselves?

Commissions for Truth and Reconciliation

3. At about the time that Nelson Mandela became president of South Africa, apartheid – the national system of racial discrimination – was officially abolished. Perhaps the greatest miracle of healing that took arose in this process was the so-called "truth commission". Functionaries who had administered apartheid, often brutally, were called upon to appear before the commission that was chaired by Archbishop Desmond Tutu. There they were asked to tell their stories in the presence of victims and the families of victims. Many of those who confessed, expressed regret and asked forgiveness for their deeds have been granted amnesty from further punishment. The world has seldom seen anything like this. What does this example teach us about healing in a world of exclusion and violence? Do you see situations in your own environment where it may be possible to establish a "truth commission"?

Acts 7:54-59   Néstor O. Míguez

*W*hen they heard these things, they became enraged and ground their teeth at Stephen. But filled with the Holy Spirit, he gazed into heaven and saw the glory of God and Jesus standing at the right hand of God. "Look", he said, "I see the heavens opened and the Son of Man standing at the right hand of God!" But they covered their ears, and with a loud shout all rushed together against him. Then they dragged him out of the city and began to stone him; and the witnesses laid their coats at the feet of a young man named Saul. While they were stoning Stephen, he prayed, "Lord Jesus, receive my spirit."

What do you make of a video game called "Stoning Stephen"? The player is a member of the crowd and has to try to hit the defenceless Christian before the others, as he continues speaking and praying. More points are scored if you hit him in the mouth and stop him talking. The sound of cheers from the crowd accompanies each successful hit. Many more points are scored if you hit him with a stone and kill him. When the final blow is dealt, the victim lets out a loud scream, the crowd applauds and sparkling lights appear on the screen.

After reading our text, this seems to be rather macabre. However, games like these are feeding the minds of millions of children and young people for several hours a day. Some of you have probably played similar games. Of course, we could make it something more palatable – there are also stories of "good" violence in the Bible: a game where young David has to aim at huge Goliath's forehead, while trying to dodge the blows from the giant's spear and sword (1 Sam. 17:50). "Good" violence and "bad" violence are leading us to believe that killing is a game, that destroying another person is a victory, that the "good people" (us) have a right to bump off "the bad people" (them, those who are different). Sadly, games prepare us for the real violence, war, torture and extermination that are taking over our world. Many video games look too much like a television news bulletin.

Violence has always been a part of our world. There have always been ways to make us believe that killing others is "natural" and necessary, that killing solves our problems. Nobody sits down in front of a video game in which, when they are about to stone a woman, a Messiah appears and says "Let anyone among you who is without sin be the first to throw a stone at her" and everybody withdraws saddened (John 8:1-11). Violence "sells", mercy is boring. This is the ideology that is gaining ground in our world, the "programme" that they are installing in our brains.

Violence is part of our human sin, it is motivated by feelings of envy, spite, fear or pride. The stone used to kill was in the heart before it was in the hand. The stones in David's sling, in the hands of those threatening the woman brought before Jesus or thrown at Stephen, were deadly weapons. However, these same stones, in other parts of the Bible, are used to build a solid house (Matt. 7:24-29). They are even used to mark the place of the mysterious appearance of God (Gen. 28:10-12). The problem is not in the stone, but in the intentions of the person who throws it, who uses it.

How often, in a nursery school, do you see toy building blocks used as symbolic weapons (by making pistols or sub-machine guns to play cops and robbers or war games) or as actual weapons, when the children throw the pieces at each other's heads. But the reverse is also true: how often is a child's imagination able to create building materials out of what seems to be rubbish or waste. Then, what were simply obstacles or useless and broken stones become living stones, cornerstones, useful for making, creating, enjoying and serving (1 Pet. 2:4-8).

Violence is not only about stones and weapons. There is violence in the hunger that results from an unjust distribution of the things that God has given us to share. There is violence in prejudice affecting those with a different skin colour or culture, or discrimination on the grounds of gender. Those forms of humanity that God himself has given us have justified many acts of violence, whether visible or invisible. These same violent statistics could be places of meeting, love, mutual enrichment and solidarity.

Because just as violence is part of our sin and comes from the heart, the ability to love, serve and protect also comes from the image of God within us, from God's love planted by faith in our hearts. This is why the prophet's promise is that the love of God will transform our hearts of stone into hearts of flesh (Eze. 11:19). Violence gives way to mercy, anger to understanding, greed to justice.

Throughout history, Christians and churches, in their various denominations, have also confused living rocks of faith with stones cast to wound and kill. Like the nursery school children, we have turned stones that the Lord gave us to build a rich and more beautiful world for his children, into things with which we use, either physically or symbolically, to attack others, casting them at their heads.

In the midst of a world that persists in finding excuses to wage wars and kill, where those who call themselves Christians, defenders of the faith, fill their hands with stones or far worse things, it becomes necessary to listen to the Word that gives life more strength than to the word that excludes and kills. We cannot be healthy while our heart continues to pump the poison of sectarianism or arrogance, while we believe ourselves to be the only bearers of healthy doctrine or superior culture.

True health, that is the path leading us towards reconciliation, comes through the recognition of others, of their pains and feelings, of their hopes and dreams, of the rich diversity with which God himself allowed the fruits of his Spirit to grow and flourish. This Spirit of God drives us to be part of God's creativity rather than to respond in zealous vengeance when we ourselves are still experiencing misunderstanding or unjust violence, when we see the consequences of poverty and injustice around us, and in many cases within ourselves. We, like Stephen, should continue speaking of the glory of God even under attack. The Spirit inspires hope for a different time, a time of glorious freedom for the children of God, even within a creation that is subjected to futility (Rom. 8:18-20).

Suggestions for use

In the group, if appropriate, or in small groups, encourage some group members to talk about any violence that they have experienced or which they have been a victim of. This must be done carefully as in some cases it can provoke strong feelings. After their stories have been told look at the reactions of the rest of the group: depression and pain, anger and a desire for vengeance, willingness to understand or forgive. Examine our feelings in light of the text we have read.

Another option would be to work on a "parable". Bring in a piece of undamaged and clean wood, some nails and a hammer. Have a pair of pliers handy as well. Invite the group members to hammer a few nails into the wood. Then reflect together on the blows, the damage to the wood (a parallel could be drawn to the Cross of Christ), then try to take the nails out – you need as much or even more force than you did to hammer them in. Finally, look at what has happened to the wood: even though the nails have been taken out, the board remains marked. However much you fill or cover the holes, the marks will always remain. Compare the experience with the issues of violence. Think about the issue of healing and reconciliation: what kind of wood are we made of? Also in this context, think about the meaning of the Resurrection.

Games. Think about games we have played recently or that we see children playing. How many of them involve forms of physical or symbolic violence? How many are based on competition? Reflect on the idea that "violence is learnt through games". Think about or invent games that do not involve violence and actually stimulate solidarity. There are groups that have websites and books dedicated to the subject. The group could investigate whether there are publications promoting "peaceful" games in your area and try to get hold of them so you can use them in the Church's teaching.

Another option is to organise a debate on the question "Is there such a thing as 'good' violence?'" – with one speaker or group defending one side and the rest, the other side – using Biblical arguments. Other sub-issues that could be raised are:

– Is there such a thing as "preventative violence"? Is that not the first form of violence?

– When does defensive violence become aggressive?

– What is the relationship between forgiveness and justice?

– In all circumstances it is good to close in a time of prayer.

Confession: when we are violent towards others, the violence is often symbolic of exclusion or disdain for their beliefs.

Seek salvation in Christ: pray for one another. Ask the Spirit to enable us to defend our faith without attacking others.

2 Samuel 13   James Poling

Some time passed. David's son Absalom had a beautiful sister whose name was Tamar; and David's son Amnon fell in love with her. Amnon was so tormented that he made himself ill because of his sister Tamar, for she was a virgin and it seemed impossible to Amnon to do anything to her. But Amnon had a friend whose name was Jonadab, the son of David's brother Shimeah; and Jonadab was a very crafty man. He said to him, "O son of the king, why are you so haggard morning after morning? Will you not tell me?" Amnon said to him, "I love Tamar, my brother Absalom's sister." Jonadab said to him, "Lie down on your bed, and pretend to be ill; and when your father comes to see you, say to him, "Let my sister Tamar come and give me something to eat, and prepare the food in my sight, so that I may see it and eat it from her hand.'" So Amnon lay down, and pretended to be ill; and when the king came to see him, Amnon said to the king, "Please let my sister Tamar come and make a couple of cakes in my sight, so that I may eat from her hand." Then David sent home to Tamar, saying, "Go to your brother Amnon's house, and prepare food for him." So Tamar went to her brother Amnon's house, where he was lying down. She took dough, kneaded it, made cakes in his sight, and baked the cakes. Then she took the pan and set them out before him, but he refused to eat. Amnon said, "Send out everyone from me." So everyone went out from him. Then Amnon said to Tamar, "Bring the food into the chamber, so that I may eat from your hand." So Tamar took the cakes she had made, and brought them into the chamber to Amnon her brother. But when she brought them near him to eat, he took hold of her, and said to her, "Come, lie with me, my sister." She answered him, "No, my brother, do not force me; for such a thing is not done in Israel; do not do anything so vile! As for me, where could I carry my shame?

And as for you, you would be as one of the scoundrels in Israel. Now therefore, I beg you, speak to the king; for he will not withhold me from you." But he would not listen to her; and being stronger than she, he forced her and lay with her. Then Amnon was seized with a very great loathing for her; indeed, his loathing was even greater than the lust he had felt for her. Amnon said to her, "Get out!" But she said to him, "No, my brother; for this wrong in sending me away is greater than the other that you did to me." But he would not listen to her. He called the young man who served him and said, "Put this woman out of my presence, and bolt the door after her." (Now she was wearing a long robe with sleeves; for this is how the virgin daughters of the king were clothed in earlier times.) So his servant put her out, and bolted the door after her. But Tamar put ashes on her head, and tore the long robe that she was wearing; she put her hand on her head, and went away, crying aloud as she went. Her brother Absalom said to her, "Has Amnon your brother been with you? Be quiet for now, my sister; he is your brother; do not take this to heart." So Tamar remained, a desolate woman, in her brother Absalom's house. When King David heard of all these things, he became very angry, but he would not punish his son Amnon, because he loved him, for he was his firstborn. But Absalom spoke to Amnon neither good nor bad; for Absalom hated Amnon, because he had raped his sister Tamar. After two full years Absalom had sheepshearers at Baal-hazor, which is near Ephraim, and Absalom invited all the king's sons. Absalom came to the king, and said, "Your servant has sheepshearers; will the king and his servants please go with your servant?" But the king said to Absalom, "No, my son, let us not all go, or else we will be burdensome to you." He pressed him, but he would not go but gave him his blessing. Then Absalom said, "If not, please let my brother Amnon go with us." The king said to him, "Why should he go with you?" But Absalom pressed him until he let Amnon and all the king's sons go with him. Absalom made a feast like a king's feast. Then Absalom commanded his servants, "Watch when Amnon's heart is merry with wine, and when I say to you, "Strike Amnon,' then kill him. Do not be afraid; have I not myself commanded you? Be courageous and valiant." So the servants of Absalom did to Amnon as Absalom had commanded. Then all the king's sons rose, and each mounted his mule and fled. While they were on the way, the report came to David that Absalom had killed all the king's sons, and not one of them was left. The king rose, tore his garments, and lay on the ground; and all his servants who were standing by tore their garments. But Jonadab, the son of David's brother Shimeah, said, "Let not my lord suppose that they have killed all the young men the king's sons; Amnon alone is dead. This has been determined by Absalom from the day Amnon raped his sister Tamar. Now there-

fore, do not let my lord the king take it to heart, as if all the king's sons were dead; for Amnon alone is dead." But Absalom fled. When the young man who kept watch looked up, he saw many people coming from the Horonaim road by the side of the mountain. Jonadab said to the king, "See, the king's sons have come; as your servant said, so it has come about." As soon as he had finished speaking, the king's sons arrived, and raised their voices and wept; and the king and all his servants also wept very bitterly. But Absalom fled, and went to Talmai son of Ammihud, king of Geshur. David mourned for his son day after day. Absalom, having fled to Geshur, stayed there three years. And the heart of the king went out, yearning for Absalom; for he was now consoled over the death of Amnon.

2 Samuel 13 is one of the most neglected stories in the Bible. Probably because of its painful topic of sexual assault, it has been left out of most churches' educational materials. Recently, women have studied the story because it relates to the personal experiences of many people. We can learn much about Christian love and ethics by studying Tamar's story and thinking about issues of justice and healing.

Tamar was the daughter of David the King, the sister of Absalom, and the half-sister of Amnon. Her life on this day revolved around her relationships with these men.[1] Amnon had sexual desire for Tamar and plotted with his uncle Jonadab to set up a situation where he could overpower and rape her. Pretending to be sick, he asked his father, King David, to send Tamar to him for comfort. Then he sent out the servants and invited her into his bed. Tamar protested by appealing to the honour of Israel and pointed out the shame they both would carry. "But he would not listen to her; and being stronger than she, he forced her and lay with her" (2 Samuel 13:14).[2] Afterward Amnon hated her and sent her away. When Tamar tore her gown and put ashes on her head to make her shame public, Absalom saw her and gave her protection in his home. David heard about what happened and was angry, yet he did nothing. Two years later, Absalom arranged a festival and had Amnon killed.

On the surface this story seems to show the horror of rape and to take a clear ethical stand against it. However, further study shows something more.

From Tamar's point of view, there are many problems. She lived in a world where men used their power to abuse others. Amnon tricked his father to get to Tamar, and then raped her. She could not protect herself. After the rape, she was emotionally destroyed. In a male-dominated culture, losing her virginity, even through rape, brought great shame. Her life was ruined, and we hear nothing more of her in the Bible.

The results of abuse are painful and long-lasting. Victims of rape suffer physically and emotionally. In addition to suffering physical injuries, they may be depressed, have trouble sleeping because of nightmares, and be afraid to engage in normal activities. Victims need special protection and care during the lengthy healing process.

Amnon was a rapist. He fed a violent desire in his heart until he acted on it. As a result he lost his humanity. He confused his desire for power and possession with sexual attraction. He used his power as a privileged male to take what he wanted by force. In a culture where men are taught to be in control of relationships, some men use their power to destroy women and children. Often no one finds out, and there are no consequences for this behaviour. Therefore it is tempting for men to abuse their power and act destructively toward women. The church needs to speak truthfully about this temptation so men will see a better way.

David was the silent bystander. He was angry that Tamar was raped, but he did not want to confront his oldest son. He had plans for the future and he did not want to change them. So his cowardice won out, and he withdrew into silence, leaving Tamar without any court of justice. He took the easy way out. In a culture where men have most of the power, men are tempted to be silent bystanders. Even though they see the harm that is done against women, they don't do anything about it. Sometimes it is easier to ignore something that is unfair than to make a big deal out of it. But silence means support of sexual violence. It is not wrong to be afraid, but it is wrong to be silent in the face of injustice. The church needs to teach men how to have courage rather than stand on the sidelines when injustice exists.

Absalom was a murderer in this story. He became so angry at Amnon that he forgot about Tamar and thought constantly of revenge. His need for revenge became more important than Tamar's need for support and comfort. Tamar was forgotten in the battle between the brothers. As a woman she had little value in the eyes of her society. A problem in many cases of rape is that male relatives act more offended than the victim. Revenge is much easier than sharing the pain of the victim. To be sympathic, one must imagine being helpless and being raped. Rather than face that pain, many men would rather imagine murdering the rapist.

Revenge repeats the abuse of the woman. She needs companions in her suffering. The church needs to help men find more constructive ways of being in solidarity with women.

The hidden message of the Tamar story is that sexual violence against women is not about their beauty or sexiness. It is about power as it is misused by men. The drama of the story is about the tension between the rapist, the silent bystander and the murderer. Meanwhile Tamar as a person is almost completely ignored.

Recently, Christian churches have become more aware of the problem of rape and sexual violence against women. In most countries, rape is against the law, and men who rape women can be punished severely. Women who have been raped can sometimes find comfort and acceptance in the church. But we have a long way to go. Too often rape is ignored, especially when it occurs in the family or the church. When a young woman named Marian told her priest that her father had raped her as a child, the priest told her to be quiet and respect her father. He said that she must be imagining things, that her father was a nice man, and that she should not bring shame on her family by telling anyone else. Later, when she was an adult, Marian met other Christians who listened to her with sympathy. They believed her story and wanted her to speak publicly about her experience. She became a powerful witness to the God who heals.

In a culture where men control most positions of power, women make easy targets for sexual abuse. Fortunately, many women today know about the dangers, and the church is listening to their cries for justice and healing. Yet there is still more work to do to help them. Women should be empowered to support one another, to believe others when they describe violent or confusing sexual experiences, and to work for justice and healing when someone has been violated.

Young men need to pay particular attention to this story. They have to make choices about what kind of man they will be. They can be like Amnon and engage in sexual abuse. They can be bystanders like David and ignore the violence against women. They can be like Absalom and seek revenge against other men while ignoring the women's need for understanding. But there are other choices. They can be friends of women and share the suffering. They can provide comfort during the long months of healing and work as partners for justice in church and society. Men can choose to work for gender justice and to end sexual violence against women.

If she had lived in another age, Tamar might have needed a strong youth programme at her church where she could talk about her feelings and find healing. Amnon and Absalom needed a church that could hold them accountable so they could not hurt anyone. Youth groups in all our churches can be safe places if we respond to the God who loves us, the God who does not want any of God's children to suffer.

Methodology

For teachers: Whenever we talk with youth about sexual violence against women and children, we need to remember that it might touch on deep pain in some group members. Often young people carry secrets about experiences of sexual violence. No one should be forced to talk about their experience if they are uncomfortable. It is important to establish an ethos of respect for all members of the class and to set boundaries on any sexual humour that might detract from the seriousness of this topic. Youth leaders need to be aware of their own issues about gender, sexuality and power so they are not surprised by the intensity of feelings that might be present in the class.

1. Opening Prayer: Begin with prayer for God's guidance in understanding this Bible story.
2. Read the story aloud (it is good if members of the class can take a turn in reading, or if everyone can read together).
3. Divide into groups of 3-4 for discussion.
   a. What happened in this story?
   b. What characters did you most identify with?
   c. What is wrong in this story? What is the tension in the plot that makes it interesting? What is the dilemma facing the characters in this story?
   d. What is the action of God in this story?
4. Hold a brief plenary discussion of above questions.
5. Make a chart on the wall with the following columns:

➤

	Tamar	Amnon	David	Absalom	God
Behaviours					
Intentions					
Consequences					
Alternative Behaviours					

    a. Ask the students to list the actual behaviours of each person. (Example: Amnon consults with his uncle about Tamar. Note: God is not active in this story.)

    b. List the intentions of these behaviours. (Example: Amnon intended to get advice on how to control Tamar)

    c. List the consequences of these behaviours. (Example: Amnon developed a plot to rape Tamar.)

    d. Finally, list the nonviolent alternatives that each character had. (Example: Amnon could have sought pastoral counseling for his obsession with Tamar and avoided coercive behaviours. Note: be careful not to place blame on Tamar as if she could have avoided this situation. Given the information she had at the time, and the limits placed on her by the culture, there was little she could have done differently.)

6. Summarize insights of the chart: All the men had choices about their behaviours that would have made things better for Tamar. Amnon could have chosen nonviolent behaviours to deal with his uncomfortable feelings of lust and desire. David could have provided support and resources for healing for Tamar and accountability for Amnon. Absalom could have provided resources for Tamar and helped the justice

system to bring accountability for Amnon. Tamar acted courageously since she trusted her father and her brother. She spoke the truth when she was vulnerable and she made the injustice known afterwards.

7. List some ethical principles for Christians on the issue of sexual violence.
   a. Violence and abuse have no place in Christian families and churches
   b. Every person deserves a safe place from violence.
   c. Every person deserves healing after sexual violence.
   d. All Christians should be advocates for education to prevent sexual violence.

8. Refer to a programme of your church that seeks to educate the people about sexual violence against women and children. Ask the students to help evaluate this programme. How could this programme be used in their own local congregations to provide more information for all members?

9. Closing Prayer: God, we thank you for preserving this story of Tamar, even though it is uncomfortable, and even painful, to read and discuss. We thank you for her courage in speaking the truth and for the insight we have gained from her witness. We ask you to give us similar courage as we become better advocates for justice and healing. In Christ's name we pray; Amen.

NOTES

[1] See Poling, The Abuse of Power, Nashville, Abingdon, 1991, pp.156-158. I am relying on the exegetical work of Phyllis Trible, Texts of Terror, pp 37ff. See also Pamela Cooper-White, The Cry of Tamar, Minneapolis, Fortress, 1995.

[2] All references are from the New Revised Standard Bible in English, Zondervan, 1989.

Genesis 21:8-21   James Poling

*T*he child grew, and was weaned; and Abraham made a great feast on the day that Isaac was weaned. But Sarah saw the son of Hagar the Egyptian, whom she had borne to Abraham, playing with her son Isaac. So she said to Abraham, "Cast out this slave woman with her son; for the son of this slave woman shall not inherit along with my son Isaac." The matter was very distressing to Abraham on account of his son. But God said to Abraham, "Do not be distressed because of the boy and because of your slave woman; whatever Sarah says to you, do as she tells you, for it is through Isaac that offspring shall be named for you. As for the son of the slave woman, I will make a nation of him also, because he is your offspring." So Abraham rose early in the morning, and took bread and a skin of water, and gave it to Hagar, putting it on her shoulder, along with the child, and sent her away. And she departed, and wandered about in the wilderness of Beer-sheba. When the water in the skin was gone, she cast the child under one of the bushes. Then she went and sat down opposite him a good way off, about the distance of a bowshot; for she said, "Do not let me look on the death of the child." And as she sat opposite him, she lifted up her voice and wept. And God heard the voice of the boy; and the angel of God called to Hagar from heaven, and said to her, "What troubles you, Hagar? Do not be afraid; for God has heard the voice of the boy where he is. Come, lift up the boy and hold him fast with your hand, for I will make a great nation of him." Then God opened her eyes and she saw a well of water. She went, and filled the skin with water, and gave the boy a drink. God was with the boy, and he grew up; he lived in the wilderness, and became an expert with the bow. He lived in the wilderness of Paran; and his mother got a wife for him from the land of Egypt.

Struggling against abuse and neglect

The Abraham saga is a sacred text for Jews, Christians and Moslems. It is a story of one family's relationship with God. Through many dangers and betrayals, they came to believe that God was faithful. The human characters were mixed up and often tried to take things into their own hands. As an actor in this story, even God is hard to understand. God ordered Abraham to send Hagar into the desert, endangering her life and the life of her unborn child. What kind of God is revealed in this story?

In the beginning of the story, Abraham and Sarah were married and had set up housekeeping.[1] God told them to leave home and head for parts unknown. Their life was full of adventure and risk. They faced famine (Gen. 12:10), threats from enemies (Gen. 12:12), conflict with family (Gen. 13:8) and war (Gen. 14:12). But the biggest threat was their childlessness. In their culture and their religious beliefs, the survival of the tribe depended on having a child. In Genesis 16, Abraham and Sarah came up with a plan to solve the problem.

The traditions of their culture allowed Abraham to take another wife in order to get an heir and save the tribe. "Sarai, Abram's wife, took Hagar, the Egyptian, her slave girl, and gave her to her husband Abram as his wife" (Gen. 16:3).[2] As soon as Hagar was pregnant, family conflict began. Being pregnant gave Hagar status above that of a slave, and Sarah was immediately jealous. With Abraham's permission, "Sarai dealt harshly with [Hagar], and she ran away from her" (Gen. 16:6).

Now we have a social justice issue, at least from a modern point of view. Even though the culture allowed a man to have more than one wife and concubine, there was no life outside the tribe. Some scholars have suggested that race and social class divided Sarah and Hagar. Hagar represents women from a social class that has few rights within the society.[3] God spoke to Hagar and sent her back to Sarah: "Return to your mistress and submit to her" (Gen. 16:9). Some scholars in the past have used this passage in an attempt to show that God approves of human slavery.

In chapter 17, God came to Abraham and Sarah and again promised a child. When Abraham pointed to Ishmael as his son, God said "No, but your wife Sarah shall bear you a son, and you shall name him Isaac... I will bless [Ishmael]... but my covenant I will establish with Isaac" (Gen. 17:19-21). In Genesis 21:9 after Isaac was born, Sarah became even more jealous of Ishmael and

Hagar and asked Abraham to cast them out of the family. God told Abraham to support Sarah, and Abraham sent Hagar and Ishmael out into the desert with only bread and water. Here God seems to approve of endangering the lives of Hagar and Ishmael.

> [Hagar] wandered about in the wilderness of Beersheba. When the water in the skin was gone, she cast the child under one of the bushes. Then she went and sat down opposite him a good way off, about the distance of a bowshot; for she said, "Do not let me look on the death of the child." And as she sat opposite him, she lifted up her voice and wept (Gen. 21:15-16).

Today we call this child abuse and neglect. It was only a miracle from God that saved Ishmael.

The usual interpretation of this story is that God is always faithful, even when our human faith is weak. But at another level, this is a story about pain and tragedy in human life. Let's focus on Hagar. She was a slave in the tribe of Abraham, a position that she did not choose. She bore a son for Abraham. But then Sarah, the powerful matriarch in the tribe, turned against her. The son, Ishmael, Abraham's heir, was rejected and condemned to die in the desert. Hagar turned her back because she could not bear to watch his suffering and death.

Some of God's actions as described in Genesis are difficult for modern people to understand. God sent Hagar back into slavery. God told Abraham to send Hagar and Ishmael into the desert. Then God rescued Hagar and Ishmael from death. Yes, God's actions are often confusing, so it is understandable when young people have questions about faith and religion. How can we live in a world where God is sometimes confusing to us? Fortunately, the last action of God was protection and healing for the persons in most danger, a theme that is repeated in many other Bible stories. But we must not fool ourselves into thinking that we always know what God is going to do. Being open and responsive to God is a difficult and risky undertaking.

Many young women in our communities share Hagar's experience. I remember a 16-year-old girl in the youth group at my church who tried to hide her pregnancy. She was ashamed and stayed away from the church and her friends. Eventually she disappeared and we heard only reports that she had moved to another state to live with relatives. She was a Hagar figure. In Chicago, where I live, there are 20,000 teenage runaways every year. Most of them leave family because they have been physically or sexually abused. Many end up on the streets of Chicago trying to survive by hustling. The Night Ministry is a program that tries to meet the needs of these young people. Churches of Chicago raise money to pay for a van and staff to provide medical advice, sexual information, counseling and protection against HIV/AIDS. They try to reach the young people soon after they come to the streets, before they lose all trust in the adult world. These young people are the Hagars and Ishmaels of our time.

But rescuing young people is not enough. We also need to understand why so many of them are in danger. Why are so many young people victims of family violence? Why is there so much sexual violence against teenagers? Why do so many youth live in situations of war and poverty? The answers are found in our understanding of gender, economics and politics. Women are less valued in most societies, and young women are often victims of sexual violence. The poor are less valued in the global economy, and young people who are poor are in danger of abuse without justice. Racial discrimination creates danger for some teenagers. Modern warfare is often directed at people who have no defenses against the violence. The church must be active in programs of social justice so that all young people have protection as they grow into adulthood. We have many stories of young people who survived difficult situations and later became leaders in their communities.

> The angel of God came to Hagar and said: What troubles you, Hagar? Do not be afraid; for God has heard the voice of the boy where he is. Come, lift up the boy and hold him fast with your hand, for I will make a great nation of him." (Gen 21:18).

All over the world, the church is involved in programmes of mercy and support for young people who suffer. The church works as a voice for justice for the poor and those in danger of violence. Whenever we become involved, we are being faithful to the God who rescued Hagar and Ishmael in the desert.

Methodology

1. Begin with prayer for God's guidance in understanding this Bible story.
2. Read the story aloud: It is good if members of the class can take a turn in reading, or if everyone can read together.　➤

---

3. Divide into groups of 3-4 for discussion.
   a. What happened in this story?
   b. What characters did you most identify with?
   c. What is wrong in this story? What is the tension in the plot that makes it interesting? What is the dilemma facing the characters in this story?
   d. What is the action of God in this story?
4. Have a brief plenary discussion of the above questions.
5. Planning for the sociodrama: Ask for volunteers who would like to act out this story for the rest of the group. Let them meet for five minutes to decide on what roles to play and how to act out the drama. Continue discussion of the above questions with the remaining members of the class.
6. Acting out the sociodrama: Ask the group to perform the story in dramatic fashion using the script from Genesis 21.
7. Discussion of sociodrama.
   a. Instruct the actors in Sociodrama to listen quietly while the group discusses what happened and how the story was interpreted.
   b. Key questions for discussion: What did you feel as you witnessed this Sociodrama? What did you observe? What key words stood out? What gestures did you notice? What happened here? How was the tension of the story resolved or not resolved? What was the attitude and behaviour of God?
   c. Debrief actors in Sociodrama. What did you feel as you acted out these roles? What were you trying to do as a character? What surprised you about your role? What did you learn from this experience?
8. Transition to contemporary experience. Our commentary says that this story might be parallel to young people today who are rejected by their families and society. The writer suggests that the church has a

➤

responsibility to provide God's care for these young people. Do you know any stories where young people are put in danger because of rejection or violence in the family, school or other places? Do you know of any church programmes that try to provide care for these young people? The teacher should be prepared with examples of programmes that provide healing for young people.

9. Questions: What is our responsibility toward young people who are rejected? What should be our church's attitude and programs? How can we understand God's action in our own lives?

10. Closing prayer. Dear God, we have been touched by your scriptures today. We thank you for Hagar and Ishmael and their faithfulness to God. We thank you for the mercy you showed them in the desert. We pray for safety for all young people today who face family violence, rejection, war or poverty. Protect them from harm and give them comfort. Help the church to become a means of love and grace for all young people. We pray all this through Jesus Christ; Amen.

NOTES

[1] See James Poling, *The Abuse of Power*, Nashville, Abingdon, 1991, pp.159-160. I am indebted to Phyllis Trible, *Texts of Terror*, Minneapolis, Fortress, 1984. Walter Brueggemann, *Genesis*, Louisville, John Knox, 1982, and Renita Weems, *Just a Sister Away: A Womanist Vision of Women's Relationships in the Bible*, Philadelphia PA, Innisfree Press, 1988.

[2] All references are from the *New Revised Standard Bible in English*, Zondervan, 1989.

[3] Renita Weems, *Just a Sister Away*. See also Trible.

4 Christian Communities in Globalized World

James 4:13 – 5:6   Néstor O. Míguez

Come now, you who say, "Today or tomorrow we will go to such and such a town and spend a year there, doing business and making money." Yet you do not even know what tomorrow will bring. What is your life? For you are a mist that appears for a little while and then vanishes. Instead you ought to say, "If the Lord wishes, we will live and do this or that." As it is, you boast in your arrogance; all such boasting is evil. Anyone, then, who knows the right thing to do and fails to do it, commits sin. Come now, you rich people, weep and wail for the miseries that are coming to you. Your riches have rotted, and your clothes are moth-eaten. Your gold and silver have rusted, and their rust will be evidence against you, and it will eat your flesh like fire. You have laid up treasure for the last days. Listen! The wages of the labourers who mowed your fields, which you kept back by fraud, cry out, and the cries of the harvesters have reached the ears of the Lord of hosts. You have lived on the earth in luxury and in pleasure; you have fattened your hearts in a day of slaughter. You have condemned and murdered the righteous one, who does not resist you.

"To his naaaaame..." shouts the preacher. "Glory!", responds a joyful congregation of very humble people with grubby children running around and young people showing signs of drug and alcohol use. The antiphone is repeated three or four times, the shouts grow stronger each time. Some people faint or go into a trance. This is a Pentecostal rally on the outskirts of a heavily-populated Latin American city. But, with only a few minor differences, similar events could also be found in Los Angeles, Cape Town or even Oslo. Elsewhere, or in those same places, similar crowds sing ancient litanies out of tune, pray their rosaries, drag their feet on pilgrimages to images of the Virgin in southern Italy or Manila. We find young Buddhists in orange-coloured robes dancing in public squares in New York or Geneva, promoting vegetarianism on the public transport in Buenos Aires. In France a conflict is emerging with young Muslim girls wanting to wear their headscarves to school. Globalization is also a religious phenomenon.

There are fast-food restaurants in most of the world's large cities. Many people, both young and old, sit down in front of computers playing online games for fun. The same sportswear brands use the same advertisements all over the world. Football is replacing traditional children's games in the heart of Africa and is the new craze on North American university campuses. The same sports channel broadcasts Formula One even for the viewers who have never set eyes on a sports car. More than half of the world's population have never used a telephone. However, their ability to feed themselves depends on calls made thousands of kilometres away. Globalization changes traditions and customs, alters how we use our free time, rushes communication, and decides whether to cut off or continue charitable aid programmes. Without noticing, it shapes our lifestyles whether we are in a small village in the south of Chile, in Mindanao or in Iceland.

When the New York Stock Exchange closes, the one in Tokyo opens, and in seconds, hundreds of millions of dollars flow from one side of the world to the other in the electronic transactions of the virtual financial market – making a fortune for a daring financial expert or bankrupting a factory employing hundreds of workers. Argentina and Brazil produce millions of tons of soya, even though it hardly features in the diet of their inhabitants, but it is their principal export. However, hundreds of thousands of children are hungry in those same countries. This too is globalization.

If on one hand we can see the public effects of globalization in the internationalization of customs or religious and cultural pluralism, the less visible effect is that the accumulation of wealth has reached its highest level ever. Never before have so few people had so much money; a minority of the world's population (less than 15 percent) consumes more than 80 percent of the available resources. Never have there been so many poor people, never has the gap been so wide between the wealth of the rich and the misery of the poor. And, thoughtless exploitation of natural resources is jeopardising the very existence of human life on the planet, even for the rich. This is the other face of globalization.

What are Christian communities doing in the light of this reality? Some take heart because the technology allows them to take the message of faith everywhere. But if this message cannot change the day-to-day reality of the 70 percent of the world's population living in poverty or help us to use the gifts of creation in a sustainable manner, these blessings will soon become a curse. James's letter, written during the 'globalization' brought on by the Roman Empire, anticipates the problems of the current Empire's globalization: the greed of those self-appointed masters of the world and of life, the accumulation of riches versus the poverty of the exploited, the corruption which prevails in a world that does not hear the voice of the righteous one.

The Christian faith was the first to think about what we now know as "globalization", the universal extension of its message. But it proposed a globalization of love, the universal calling to the grace and justice of God. The current globalization of inequalities, cultural impositions and rapid earnings at the cost of the poor is its exact opposite. This is why James was already warning that those who work like that make themselves enemies of the love of God.

Being a community that heals and reconciles is, therefore, being a community of the "other" globalization, the globalization proposed by the Holy Spirit, that is coupled with hope, that expresses itself through charity, that respects identities and proposes ways of justice; a community that can raise up prophetic voices, like James's, to warn against impending destruction should we bind ourselves to the globalization of accumulation and injustice. We are called, therefore, to globalize the message and the practices that return humankind to obedience of the God of love, to a willingness to serve, to the enjoyment of shared living: that is the healing and reconciliatory work of the Spirit.

Suggestions for use

This issue can also help us with intergenerational dialogue (which is another thing that technological globalization tends to destroy). Young people could talk to their parents, grandparents, relatives and older friends, also in the Church, to discover what customs and cultural aspects have changed in the last generation. Then we can ➤

make a list to see how globalization has affected the life of this community.

After making the list, note on one side the benefits of each change, and then the bad things that it could have caused. We may note that in some cases the same situations are considered beneficial for some and harmful for others. Or that some of the supposedly "good" things end up having a destructive effect on the life of the community.

Lastly, look at the passage in James 4:13-5:7. What criteria does the apostle use to differentiate the good things from the bad things?

The discussion could provide an indication of how we, as communities, can help a globalization of justice, even for local issues.

Another option would be to ask the young people to collect pictures, posters, or print or television advertisements, for "international", global products and analyse them to find out what values they bring. This could lead to a debate on what is hidden behind "globalized" culture. Then we could see if these are the values and practices denounced by James. An interesting example could be clothing, which is one of the most internationalized products, but one which James condemns to rot.

How can we offer a Gospel "counterculture"? How would we go about advertising "universal grace"?

5 *Proclaiming Hope*

Matthew 14:22-33   Nina Lundgren

*I*mmediately *he made the disciples get into the boat and go on ahead to the other side, while he dismissed the crowds. And after he had dismissed the crowds, he went up the mountain by himself to pray. When evening came, he was there alone, but by this time the boat, battered by the waves, was far from the land, for the wind was against them. And early in the morning he came walking toward them on the sea. But when the disciples saw him walking on the sea, they were terrified, saying, "It is a ghost!" And they cried out in fear. But immediately Jesus spoke to them and said, "Take heart, it is I; do not be afraid." Peter answered him, "Lord, if it is you, command me to come to you on the water." He said, "Come". So Peter got out of the boat, started walking on the water, and came toward Jesus. But when he noticed the strong wind, he became frightened, and beginning to sin, he cried out, "Lord, save me!" Jesus immediately reached out his hand and caught him, saying to him, "You of little faith, why did you doubt?" When they got into the boat, the wind ceased. And those in the boat worshipped him, saying, "Truly you are the Son of God".*

* Read the following summary of the story to your group:

The story begins with Jesus asking his disciples to go aboard the boat and sail ahead of him to the other side of the Lake of Galilee. He has just performed a miracle: 5000 men, in addition to women and children, had been fed. He needed to be alone for a while, so that is why he sent his disciples before him.

When the evening came, he was alone. The boat was now far out in the middle of the lake, tossed by the waves, for the wind was blowing against the boat.

Jesus saw that the disciples were afraid, very afraid, when they saw him coming towards them on the water. Jesus calmed their fear, and he challenged Peter to join him on the water.

Peter went out of the boat and walked towards Jesus, and as long as he had his focus on Jesus he walked on the water without a problem. But when Peter realized he saw how strong the wind was, he became afraid, and Peter started to sink.

He called out for Jesus to help him, and Jesus did.

How did he dare to step out of the boat and walk on the water?

He was a fisherman, who had lived his whole life by the water. He had respect for the water, he knew how dangerous it could be. But he stepped out of the boat anyway.

Why?

Because Jesus called for him, and if there was anyone that Peter felt he could trust and feel secure with, it was Jesus. And something else: Peter saw Jesus' hand, and he knew that, whatever happened, Jesus would reach out and help him.

But suddenly Peter had started to doubt his ability; he started to think about just relying on himself, and that made him scared, because he realized that it was not possible for him to walk on water. And suddenly he started to sink, and he didn't see Jesus' hand anymore, and then he yelled, "Help Me, Jesus!"

And what did Jesus do? He stretched out his hand even farther, to show Peter that he was still there. And he grabbed Peter's hand and took him back into the boat.

But he also asked Peter, "Why didn't you trust me? Why did you loose your faith? Where were your hopes? Why didn't you see my hand anymore?"

Jesus wanted Peter to realize that hecontinued to be there for him.

Jesus wants us to realize that he is there for us. Even if we are way out on the sea, or in some other kind of trouble, he is there to give us hope, he is prepared to support us with his hands.

He doesn't leave us to ourselves at any time, but sometimes we don't see his hands, we don't realize he's there right by our side. Because we have closed our eyes. We don't want to see that he is there. We have already decided that it's no use to try doing anything more or different from what is normal, because we think it will only cost us more than we can pay.

It seems too much of a problem to go outside the normal limits that keep us safe. It might be a temptation to our enemies. We would be taking a risk. Are we willing to do that?

Things to talk about!

Have you ever done anything that you were not sure you could handle?

Has anybody asked you to do something you thought was too difficult?

Have you asked anyone to do anything like that for you?

If anyone asked you to do something scary for them, would you?

If you answer "yes": Why would you do it?

If you answer "no": Why not?

Is there anyone you feel you can always trust?

What is trust?

What makes a person "trustworthy"?

Are you a trustworthy person?

What do you think Jesus meant when he said to Peter, "O you of little faith" (Matt. 14:31)?

And how do you think Peter felt when Jesus reached out his hand to him?

What is hope?

Has anyone ever given you hope?

Have you ever given anyone hope?

How can you let a person know that you care without speaking?

How can you use your hands to show someone that you care?

How can we learn to see when someone is reaching out their supportive hands to us?

How can we tell when someone wants to help us?

Is helping someone else part of what it means to give them hope?

Things to do!

Let the children sit in a circle with their eyes shut, holding hands.

Ask one child to press the hand of the neighbour on his or her right side, and ask each child in turn to send this pressing, hand by hand, around the circle until it comes back to the original child. Do this without any sound.

Let the children organize themselves in pairs.

Tell them that one person in each pair is supposed to have his or her eyes shut, and let the other one lead them around the room. Do that for a while, and then tell the two children in each pair to change positions. After awhile you could ask them to make some small changes in the room (rearranging the furniture, for example), and make the area more difficult to walk through. There could be something to climb over or under, there might be some stairs to walk up and down, and so on. Perhaps you will have the opportunity to go outside. This will depend on your surroundings.

Let everyone stand in a circle very close to each other, almost shoulder to shoulder.

One child is in the middle. The person in the middle is supposed to feel so sure and trustful of his or her friends that he/she, with eyes shut, lets himself or herself lean round in the circle, supported by the hands of the other children. The children in the circle are to make sure he or she never falls. In the beginning the circle can be very narrow and then, after the group feels more secure, the circle can grow somewhat wider.

Let them create a drama, acting out one or more situations from their own lives when they have felt hope because of someone's actions, or when they felt they could share hope with someone else.